CIT 5 6/08

LECTURES ON ECONOMIC PRINCIPLES

VOLUME I

LECTURES ON
ECONOMIC PRINCIPLES

VOLUME I

SIR DENNIS H. ROBERTSON

Emeritus Professor of Political Economy in the University of Cambridge

> '*It's too late to correct it,*' *said the Red Queen:* '*when you've once said a thing, that fixes it, and you must take the consequences.*'
>
> **THROUGH THE LOOKING-GLASS**

STAPLES PRESS LIMITED
LONDON

FIRST PUBLISHED 1957

Copyright © 1957

by Sir Dennis Robertson

This book is set in 'Monotype' Caslon Old Face series

Made and printed in England by
STAPLES PRINTERS LIMITED
at their Rochester, Kent, establishment

PREFACE

If I had thought the publishers would agree, I would, I think, have suggested demoting the sober title of this little series to the rank of sub-title, and using as main title the words 'Rightly or Wrongly'. Rightly or wrongly, this is what I told them, – those young men and women, mostly, though not exclusively, in the second of their three years of economic study, who attended (with varying regularity) my lectures on Economic Principles at Cambridge in the years 1945–6 to 1956–7. And if it was all wrong, it can't be helped now.

The configuration of the academic year dictated the arrangement of the lectures into three groups, two of about sixteen lectures each and one of twelve or thirteen; and that general arrangement has been preserved in this series, the division between chapters sometimes conforming to, but sometimes departing from, the division between lectures, – truth does not always go nicely into fifty-minute slabs. The present volume deals with introductory matters and with the Theory of Value; its successors will deal respectively with the Theory of Distribution and with Money and the fluctuations of economic activity. All this sounds very old-fashioned, I know: but, for good or evil, that is how it was.

Limitation of time compelled me to confine my treatment to a closed system with no international contacts, and to omit any but the most incidental reference to Public Finance. Even so, there was need for rigorous selection and compression, especially in the short summer term, when the conflict between time available and my own interest in the subject-matter was most acute.

I am most anxious therefore that this gathering together of dead bones should not be mistaken for an attempt to write a well-balanced textbook covering the whole field of economics, still less for an attempt at a comprehensive treatise. I hope it will be taken for what it was, – an attempt to contribute, according to my lights, to a complex and progressive three-year curriculum in which a number of brains and voices were involved besides my own.

This consciousness of membership of an orchestra, and a not wholly harmonious one at that, probably affected my handling of the problems of selection and emphasis in two contrasting ways. On the one hand I felt justified in treating with a brevity out of accord with their intrinsic importance a whole range of questions connected with the structure of industry on which I had nothing special to say and felt complete confidence in the expositions, printed and oral, available to my class. On the other hand I felt impelled to give what may seem *sub specie aeternitatis* to have been excessive attention to certain matters on which I felt myself to be swimming against a stream and to be the custodian of a viewpoint in danger of neglect. New orthodoxies can be at least a tyrannous as old ones.

In preparing the lectures for print I have had two imaginary critics looking over my shoulder. One keeps saying 'Such sloppy and inaccurate treatment may have been pardonable in a routine lecture; but you ought to have revised it thoroughly before going into print'. The other – a student possessed of a photographic memory or a fantastic capacity for note-taking – keeps protesting 'It's all very well to write that now, but it isn't what you actually *said* to us, you know'. I have tried to hold the balance sensibly between them, with valued help from Dr A. R. Prest, who has kindly read the typescript but bears no responsibility for what continues to appear in the final text.

Readers of these volumes who have been kind enough to read my two collections of essays published since the

war, *Utility and All That* (Allen and Unwin, 1952) and
Economic Commentaries (Staples Press, 1956), must
naturally be prepared to find a certain amount of repeti-
tion of matter with which they are already acquainted.
They are asked to take an indulgent view of this, as
Messrs Allen and Unwin have kindly consented to do.

It has seemed inappropriate to clutter a text of this
kind with footnotes. I can only hope that a sentence here
and there, together with the reading lists, will be or would
have been taken as sufficient acknowledgment by all those,
alive and dead, from whom I have committed piracy.

D. H. R.

Cambridge.
September 1957.

CONTENTS

I

WHAT IS ECONOMICS?

These lectures are intended primarily for those who are in the second of three years of economic study; but it is my desire that they should also be intelligible to those who are approaching the subject for the first time, while I am not without hope that parts of them at least may be of some interest to those whom the Prayer-book describes as of riper years. I shall begin at the beginning, if only because it is so difficult to think of anywhere else to begin; but I shall feel free to reach rather difficult matters rather quickly. If some people feel they have heard all this before, and others that they are being dragged somewhat roughly up the mountain, I hope both classes will try to feel forbearance towards each other and towards myself.

There is one important limitation on the scope of the lectures to which I want to draw attention at once. For reasons of time, I have to confine myself to what is called a closed system; that is to say I shall have to omit, except for occasional incidental references, all the complications arising out of international trade and other international economic transactions. In view of the outstanding part played by these complications in the problems of the world, and especially of this country, you may well think this is rather like a performance of *Hamlet* without the Prince of Denmark: but there it is, and you will be hearing plenty about these problems from others.

It may be useful if I say something about books. I don't regard it as my function to prescribe a list of reading, — that is rather for your supervisors, in the light of your very various needs and situations. But I must make certain assumptions: and the chief assumption I shall make is that you are being advised to read in due course all or a substantial part of the best-known book of each of the three great Cambridge economists, – Marshall's *Principles*, Pigou's *Economics of Welfare* and Keynes's *General Theory of Employment, Interest and Money*. I will say a little about each of them.

Marshall's work is over sixty years old, and parts of it naturally bear evidence of that fact. But nobody has ever succeeded in replacing it, and every time I look at it I am astonished again at its freshness and wisdom. But it is a deceptive book. Here is what Pigou said about it in an address delivered soon after Marshall's death. 'The first time one reads the *Principles* one is very apt to think that it is all perfectly obvious. The second time one has glimpses of the fact that one does not understand it at all. If then one reads some other book on the same subject and comes back to it, one discovers at the third or fourth reading that in those platitudinous sentences difficulties are faced and solved that elsewhere are not perceived at all or are slurred over. One discovers behind the smooth sentences, which hide it like a façade, an engine of polished steel. . . . When one discovers that one did not know beforehand everything that Marshall has to say, one has taken the first step towards becoming an economist!'

But Marshall's book, even over the range with which it deals – and in reading it it is important to remember that it was intended as the first volume of three or four – needs supplementing on certain topics; and the book which comes nearest to supplementing it satisfactorily is, I think, Chamberlin's *Theory of Monopolistic Competition*. I therefore add that to the books most or a good part of which I assume you will be reading. I shall be dealing this term with the range of subjects covered by Marshall, Books I to V, and by Chamberlin; next term with the subject-matter of Marshall, Book VI.

Of Pigou's own book, as of Marshall's, it is true that it varies very greatly in difficulty. There is a somewhat formidable group of chapters near the beginning, about the national dividend, by which it is important not to get held up, but to press on. If I *have* a criticism of the book it is that in his anxiety to show the application of his analysis to real life Pigou has been over-lavish with his factual illustrations, which sometimes extend to great length; and once more it is important not to get bogged down, but to get through the flesh at the bones. Roughly speaking, Parts I and II deal with topics which I shall be reaching this term and Parts III and IV with topics which I shan't reach till next term. There is much to be said for reading Pigou's small book *Income* as an introduction to his habits of thought.

Keynes's celebrated book is of a different character. Much of it is brilliantly written, though some of it is very difficult. And much of it is still highly controversial. When I am within sight of reaching the topics with which it deals, which won't be till much later in the year, I shall suggest that you should couple your reading of it with the reading of one or two critical studies that have been made of it. But I think I will also mention from the start, as a fifth main plank for your platform, Haberler's book *Prosperity and Depression*, – a more general book covering the same line of country (use the 1941 edition or the 1939 edition with a separately bound supplement).

In addition to these five books, I shall, as I approach various topics, make supplementary mention of books, or parts of books, and articles which I myself have found useful and believe that others who wish and have time to go more deeply into these topics will find useful. It will be better, I think, to proceed in this piecemeal way than to deluge you from the start with one enormous miscellaneous list.[1]

If we are going to begin at the beginning, we had better

[1] [The suggestions in which, so far as the contents of this volume are concerned, these threats materialised are printed as an appendix to this chapter.]

ask what Economics is. English economists, unlike Continental ones, have never set much store by matters of definition and terminology; and no doubt it is true, in this matter as in others, that the nature of the pudding is best discovered by eating it. Nevertheless it is quite a good thing even for those of us who have made some progress with the meal to lay down our spoons from time to time and take stock of where we have got to.

The first thing to notice is that about three-quarters of a century ago our subject quietly changed its name. You are reading for the Economics Tripos; but I am an anachronism, – I am called a professor of Political Economy. This older term can perhaps best be defined by literal translation as State Housekeeping; the old Political Economy could be thought of as being primarily a body of maxims for statesmen. The newer term 'economics' brings out two things: (1) the termination -ics indicates that our study is or aspires to be a science, like physics, dynamics and so forth; (2) the dropping of the word 'political' emphasises that our ultimate concern is with individual human beings, not with 'States'. But while economics thus is or aims at being a branch of objective study, it is a branch which in sheer intellectual interest is inferior, or so I think most people would admit, to many others which are open to our pursuit. When one considers the wonders of modern physics or the glories of ancient Greek or modern English literature, one is driven to the conclusion that as an intellectual pastime economics is rather a drab and second-rate affair. If it is worth pursuing – and it certainly *is* – it is mainly worth pursuing not for its own sake, but with a practical object.

What is that object? Not personal enrichment, – some famous economists have died rich, but most have not – and are not likely to. On the other hand the acquisition of a mental training, and of a body of knowledge, which will be of use in a business career is a common motive for undertaking the study of economics, and an entirely legitimate one, provided that not too much is expected. It can't be too clearly understood that, in this university at least, the course in economics in no sense purports to be a training in business method or administration; provided that *is* understood, the prospective business man can fairly hope to get from it two things, — a useful equipment of facts about the real world, and a technique of thinking which, whether or not he can often apply it directly to his problems, should enable him to approach them from a broader point of view and to see more clearly his own relation to the whole set-up of which he will form a part.

But not all students of economics are aiming at a business career. And for the rest — and perhaps for the prospective business man too — the main practical object in undertaking the study of economics is surely this, — the formation of *judgments*, which one can bring to bear according to one's opportunities — as employer, as civil servant, as minister of religion, or just as ordinary citizen and voter — on proposals for the promotion of human welfare, proposals some, though by no means all, of which involve political action.

Well, after that little piece of sermonising about the nature of our subject, can we proceed to define its scope? It is difficult, I think, to improve on Marshall's famous definition as 'the study of mankind in the ordinary business of life'. It is not precise, — no useful definition can be; but it brings out two things, — that we are concerned with man, and that we are concerned with him in only some of his many aspects. Perhaps, however, we can learn more by taking another definition, given by Marshall's contemporary Cannan. Economics, says Cannan, is the 'study of the things having to do with man's material welfare'. In what does this, the material welfare of man, consist?

Not, we don't need telling, in money alone. Nor in

material objects alone; our landlady when she sweeps our room, the professional pianist when he plays to us, contribute to our material welfare. The latter must be conceived as a flow of enjoyment or satisfaction derived from the good things of life. But not as consisting in all the possible kinds of satisfaction. Ruskin, enraged at what he regarded as the narrow conception of wealth prevalent among the economists of a hundred years ago, cried out in protest 'There is no wealth but life'. But that protest goes too far, and to act on it would make our study unmanageable. We must limit ourselves to the more material and less spiritual parts or aspects of welfare. This is admittedly a hazy boundary-line. 'We shall never be able to say of any man', says Cannan, 'that 50 per cent of his welfare comes from food, clothing, shelter, pictures and concerts [note Cannan's inclusion of these among the sources of material welfare], 25 per cent from the love of his wife, 15 per cent from his support of his Church, and 10 per cent from his pride of his position as president of the local party caucus.' But vague as the line is, we need have no doubt that it is worth while having a separate science of economics to deal with the more material parts of welfare; for to quote an older economist still, Adam Smith, 'the subdivision of employment in philosophy, as well as in every other business, improves dexterity and saves time'. And we economists are fortunate compared with our fellow social scientists in that economic affairs seem to be more capable of scientific treatment than most parts of human conduct, because the motives at work are on the whole more regular and more persistent.

Material welfare, then, is not the same as total welfare; and sometimes the pursuit of the one may conflict with the pursuit of the other. Nevertheless, as it seems to me, we can reasonably plan our studies on the working hypo-thesis laid down by my predecessor in this chair, Pigou: 'when we have ascertained the effect of any cause on economic welfare, we may, unless of course there is special evidence to the contrary, regard this effect as *probably* equivalent in direction, though not in magnitude, to the effect on total welfare.' And in pursuing our studies so planned we can pay heed to a piece of advice given by my grandparent in this chair, Alfred Marshall, so good that I propose to read it at length. 'The less we trouble ourselves with scholastic enquiries as to whether a certain consideration comes within the scope of economics the better. If the matter is important, let us take account of it as far as we can. . . . If it is one on which the general machinery of economic analysis and reasoning cannot get any grip, then let us leave it aside in our purely economic studies . . . remembering always that some sort of account of it must be taken by our ethical instincts and our common sense, when they as ultimate arbiters come to apply to practical issues the knowledge obtained and arranged by economics and other sciences.'

Nevertheless two important stretches of the frontier between what is economics and what is not have become so inflamed since our mentors wrote the words which I have just quoted that something more must be said about them. What is the relation between economic welfare and (1) work, (2) national security and power?

(1) Clearly as economists we are concerned not only with the flow of satisfaction derived from the good things of life, but with the toil and pain that go to their making. I gave you just now Ruskin's definition of wealth; here is the definition given by another critic of the old Political Economy, the anonymous author of a certain open letter to Lord John Russell, written in 1821. 'Wealth is liberty,' he writes, 'liberty to recreation – liberty to enjoy life – liberty to improve the mind. Wealth is disposable time, and nothing more.' That again, like Ruskin's definition, is obviously too strong. Leisure is certainly not the whole of welfare, and perhaps is best not even described as *part*

B

of welfare. But it is certainly an indispensable *means* to welfare; and welfare, as we shall see later, can often be usefully conceived as a kind of *net balance* of satisfactions achieved over dissatisfactions incurred, by work and in other ways, in achieving them.

But that is not the whole of the story. The trouble is that work also, even though undertaken, as we say, 'for' reward, is itself up to a point a direct source of welfare. In particular, it is now generally recognised that the evil of complete and prolonged unemployment consists not only in loss of income but in loss of *status*, in the feeling of being unwanted, – an evil which is not removable either by doles or even by the provision of obviously 'made' work. Now over a large range the objectives of what is now officially called 'high and stable employment' and of high industrial efficiency and output coincide; but over a certain range they may conflict. For instance in the siting of new industrial plants in this country a question of policy arises as to how much attention should be paid to geographical factors and transport facilities on the one hand, and how much on the other to the desirability of preventing the re-emergence of massed unemployment in what used to be called the depressed areas. And attached as it were to this main question of policy there is a minor question of pedagogics: if and in so far as the objective of high employment is being given primacy, are we to say that one sort of economic welfare is being sacrificed to another, or are we to say that economic welfare in general is being curtailed for a non-economic end? I do not feel sure of the answer to this pedagogical question; nor do I think the question of policy can be answered in general and decisive terms. But I would go so far as to say that in situations of this kind the economist has a special duty to act as watchdog for economic welfare in the narrower sense in which it depends on high efficiency and high output, since if *he* doesn't nobody else will!

(2) National *safety* and *survival* are prerequisites for the enjoyment of economic welfare. Further, while as moralists we might like to deny that national *strength* and *power* can be and often are used to promote the economic welfare of the members of national groups, we should find it very hard honestly to do so. Conversely, in war and states of near-war, economic resources are used on a vast scale to feed the furnaces of national power: and power, from a means to welfare, tends to become elevated into an end in itself, – no longer, to quote some words of Hawtrey, 'an occasional intruder into the fair field of utility' but a chronic rival to welfare as an object of economic activity. What is to be the attitude of the economist to all this? Clearly he cannot just hide his head in the sand. In certain matters of accountancy, as we shall see when we come to discuss the national income, it may be best for him to treat Power *as if* it were Welfare, even though he knows it isn't. And in giving his advice, he cannot and should not, in my view, unless impelled by overriding ethical motives, deny the claims of Power. But in this matter too, as in the case of Employment, it would seem that he has a special duty to think and act as a watchdog for welfare in a sense of that word which is less than coextensive with *all* the aims which are set up as goals for human endeavour.

The nature of economics can perhaps be made plainer by considering its relation with certain other studies, using an analogy taken from its own field. The miller takes over his raw material from the farmer, works it up with the aid of the products of the engineer, and hands over the finished product to the baker. So the economist takes his data from one group of studies, uses tools furnished by a second group, and hands over his results to be dealt with by a third. Let us look at these groups in turn.

The first group contains (1) the whole body of the *Natural Sciences*, which can be regarded for this purpose as a single whole. Evidently man's material welfare depends on the degree of victory which he has achieved in his struggle with Nature; economic life and structure are continually being profoundly affected by technical change. Historians in recent years have rightly emphasised that many of the features of modern capitalism, including the factory system itself, can be traced back beyond that great outburst of technical change which we call the Industrial Revolution and whose beginning we place somewhere about 1760. But it remains true that for the last two hundred years man has been living in a whirlwind of scientific discovery and achievement for which there is no precedent in his previous history, and that each new phase of this tumultuous development modifies the shape of his economic environment. And the end, as we know, is not yet. To give just one out of a myriad possible examples, the progressive substitution of electrical for steam power in recent decades has been affecting not only the total sum of economic welfare, but such special matters as the local distribution of industry between national units and between town and countryside. The economist can't be a master of the natural sciences, pure or applied; but the livelier his idea of what they are up to the better.

The technologist on his side, whether he be engineer, nutrition expert or what not, is not as well qualified as he sometimes supposes to pronounce on problems of *general* economic welfare, not always realising how much the latter depends on *choosing* between alternative uses of limited total resources. Indeed some economists, in an endeavour to draw more sharply the line between economics and technology, have rejected as too wide and flabby definitions of economics which link it up with material welfare, and have proposed such definitions as this (which is due to Professor Robbins): economics is 'the science which studies human behaviour as a relationship between ends and scarce means which have alternative uses'. It seems to me that such a definition is at once too narrow and too wide, excluding from the scope of economics such topics as the defects of organisation which lead to a general underemployment of resources; and procuring the exclusion of the chemist and the engineer only to admit the army commander and the cricket captain placing his field, both of whom are concerned with allocation of scarce means which have alternative uses. All the same this definition does, as we shall see, cover a good part of economic analysis, and the line which it seeks to draw between economics and technology must be drawn somewhere, if not by definition then by common sense.

We pass on, still within Group I, to (2) *Psychology*, the science of the workings of the human mind. When the economist talks about cause and effect, he usually means that things will so work on people's minds as to induce them to act in certain ways: so he ought to have some idea how minds work. Now psychology itself is a fluid and controversial subject, and it is not easy for the economist to keep up with it. He has often been accused of using a crude and obsolete psychology, assuming without good cause that in the ordinary business of life men seek their own interests, and seek them intelligently, whereas it is clear in fact that, in the first place, they often act unreflectingly, under the influence of sudden impulse or of ingrained custom, and secondly, that they are often influenced by altruism or public spirit. How damaging is this charge to the fabric of economic theory? That you must each decide for yourselves, in the light of your developing knowledge both of the content of economic theory and of the real world. But I will remind you of two familiar points. First, actions which appear to be purely automatic and unreflecting, such as putting on one's clothes or navigating a bicycle, are often based upon elaborate previous experience and experiment, conducted either by the individual or the race. Secondly, economics does not lay down the law as to *why* people want to make good bargains, — whether it is to benefit themselves or others, — whether it is to acquire wealth, or power, or fame, or simply, so to speak, as a certificate of effective work. So that perhaps it doesn't go far wrong in assuming that *while at business* – the man in the factory or the office, the woman shopping for the family (or perhaps nowadays the other way round) – most people are usually fairly rational egoists, though their rationality is tempered by custom and their egoism by codes, varying from group to group, of what is or is not done.

Nevertheless, especially if his special field of interest is the administration of industry or the management of labour, the economist must do what he can to keep his psychology up to date, and to learn what he can about what is being discovered, by observation and experiment, about the efficacy of non-financial stimuli to enterprise and toil, whether they be Orders of the Bath, music while you work, inter-factory competitions or broadcast appeals by Cabinet Ministers to ensue the public welfare. But he had better, I think, keep hanging about the back of his mind some very wise words of Marshall, to the effect that 'progress mainly depends on the extent to which the strongest, and not merely the highest, forces of human nature can be utilised for the increase of social good'.

(3) I turn to the third member of our first group, *Law*. Man in his business life is largely affected by the framework of law within which he operates, and the economist must know something about it. Of the laws governing the possession and disposition of *property* I will say a little more presently in another connection. Important also to the economist is the threefold attitude of the law

towards *contracts*. Normally it enforces the fulfilment of contracts freely made between persons. But there are some contracts which it forbids altogether, e.g., in this country, contracts to hire people to work in certain trades at less than certain wages, or to hire women to work in mines. And finally there are certain classes of contract, namely those held to be 'in restraint of trade', about which the English common law traditionally takes up an intermediate position, not forbidding them but declining to enforce them between the parties concerned. This fact probably had a good deal of influence on the different forms taken by industrial monopoly in different countries in the latter part of the nineteenth century. In Germany the readiness of the law to enforce such contracts furthered the growth of those associations of producers, retaining a good deal of their independence, which are known as cartels; in England and America the uncertainty whether such contracts would be enforced helped to cause monopoly, where it developed, to take rather the form of complete fusion of interests. But in more recent years some strange findings of the English courts have a good deal altered the position; restrictive agreements of one kind and another have now become common in this country as well, and, as you know, a new law dealing with them is just coming into operation.

II

We come to our second group of subjects, – those which economics uses as its tools. The first of these is (1) *Logic*, or the science of reasoning. The economist uses, so far as he can, the same 'inductive' method as the natural scientist; that is, he collects and observes facts, frames generalisations on the basis thereof, and tests these as far as possible before using them as a basis for prediction. But he is much worse placed than the natural scientist, though not than other types of social scientist, for carrying out this procedure. This is due first to the extreme variety and uncertainty of the behaviour of his material, human nature, as compared with that of gases or even guinea-pigs; and secondly to his inability – unless he happens also to be a commissar – to conduct controlled experiments, shutting out the operation of all forces except that which he desires to isolate for observation. Nevertheless the work of economics on the inductive side is now at last making considerable strides.

The economist's work, however, consists also in 'deduction', i.e. in taking his generalisations such as they are and manipulating and combining them so as to draw inferences not obvious at first sight. This work is highly important and productive, and by no means to be scoffed at, as it sometimes is, as 'mere theorising': but its nature must be understood. In one sense you can't get more out of a proposition, any more than out of a pint pot, than there was in it to start with; and propositions of pure economics, like the propositions of Euclid, are nothing but glorious tautologies in the sense that, given certain axioms, the final result was all wrapped up in the starting-point for anyone with sufficient intuition to see it there. But such intuition – such power to see at a glance the whole implications of a situation without going through the process of unwinding – is, according to St Thomas Aquinas, one of the marks distinguishing angels from men; and no mere man need be ashamed of spending a reasonable proportion of his time and wits in deductive reasoning.

It is perhaps not superfluous even now to comment on the popular tendency to mistake the nature of economic 'laws'. Like those of other sciences, they are of course *statements* of general tendencies, not *commands*, – this use of the word 'law' being presumably theological or poetical in origin. ('Kill not for pleasure of killing, and seven times never kill man', says the poet Kipling in enunciating the 'law of the jungle' taught to Mowgli, where the prosaic scientist would have observed 'Wolves seldom kill for the sake of killing; they very seldom attack man'.)

Hence it is impossible to 'break' or 'disobey' economic laws. But two things *are* possible. One is that certain individuals or groups – a St Francis and his followers at one end of the scale, an Al Capone and his fellow gangsters at the other – should constitute an exception, of greater or less importance, to economic generalisations. The other is that individuals or groups should decline to regulate their conduct in the light of such generalisations, for instance by attempting to charge too much for their goods or their labour. In this case they will tend to get into trouble, like Elpenor the companion of Odysseus, who ignored the law of gravity (you will remember that he took too much to drink and went to sleep on the roof and when he woke up, in Homer's words, 'forgot to go down by the stairs' but walked over the edge and broke his neck).

Marshall's definition of an economic law is framed in two stages. A social law, he says, is a statement that a certain course of action may be expected under certain conditions from the members of a social group. And economic laws are those social laws which relate to branches of conduct in which the strength of the motive chiefly concerned can be measured by a money price. I have never been quite happy about this definition, for two reasons. First, as I shall illustrate later on, the operation of economic laws is not confined to societies which use money, and I would rather express the difference between economic and other social laws in terms of our old concept of 'material welfare'. But secondly, it is doubtful whether the definition leaves room for the most famous of all economic laws, the so-called 'law of diminishing return' in all its various forms, which will much concern us later. Economic laws are not solely, though doubtless they are mainly, statements of how *men* tend to behave; they include also statements of what tends to happen when man gets mixed up with inanimate objects in his quest for economic welfare.

I pass on to the second subject in Group II, (2) *Mathematics*. The economist is concerned with questions of greater or less, so mathematical methods have their place in his armoury. So far as his abilities permit, he should use the weapons of Statistics, — the science of making figures speak, of getting the most out of crude numerical data by systematic arrangement and treatment; for this is the best substitute at his disposal for the method of controlled experiment from which he is debarred. And in his deductive work, since his questions are largely of the nature 'what will make X as great as possible?', it follows that if he understands the language of the differential calculus he will easily see its bearing, and if he doesn't he *may* find it worth while to acquire its elements, and *will* find it worth while to wield the imperfect substitute of simple co-ordinate geometry, which is used in most textbooks and of which I shall make a moderate use, without further explanation, in these lectures. The economist who is *not* mathematically minded need not be down-hearted: he will see some things less quickly and less securely than the mathematician; but he will also be immune from the temptation to which the latter is subject to press refinements of deductive reasoning beyond what is useful. All economists, I think, whether mathematically minded or not, should acquire the habit of 'quantitative imagination', — of asking themselves suddenly 'Now what is the *order of size* of this thing — national income, skilled wage rate, quantity of bank deposits, or whatever it may be — of which I have been talking?'

III

As our Group III, the subjects to which economics hands

its data as *their* raw material, we come back to our old friends (1) *Ethics* and (2) *Politics*, which I will treat together, and define for the purpose in hand as the study of how people think they ought to behave, both as individuals and as members or officers of organised communities. On this I have little to add to what I have already said. We can start, as I have suggested, by taking Pigou's working hypothesis that anything which promotes economic welfare promotes also, though not perhaps in the same degree, total welfare. Nevertheless the economist must be prepared to see some suggested course of action which he thinks would promote economic welfare turned down – his own judgment perhaps consenting, perhaps not – for overriding reasons: on the ground, as in the case for instance of the removal of a protective duty on steel, that it would impair national security; or on the ground, as in the case of an issue of lottery bonds, that it would encourage bad habits of mind; or simply on the ground, as in the case for instance of some ingenious scheme for family allowances or for a capital levy, that it would be administratively top-heavy and impracticable.

A more difficult practical question faces the economist if he judges that a certain course of action would promote economic welfare if public opinion would accept it, but will on balance damage even economic welfare if public opinion won't accept it. For instance an economist might come to the conclusion that, in a pronounced slump, either a general cut in money wages or a large programme of public works would *per se* promote employment; but that if the trade unions react against the former by calling a general strike, or big business against the latter by curtailing capital outlay, the last state of employment and output will be worse than the first. With how much insistence is he to parade and press the results of his 'purely economic' analysis? Evidently there is no clear-cut answer. On the one hand he must avoid breaking his head uselessly against brick walls; on the other he must remember that the gradual encroachment of ideas is very powerful, perhaps more powerful even than prejudice and vested interest, in the long run.

Let me recapitulate very briefly what I have been trying to say. Economics is the study of mankind in the ordinary business of life, or of the more material part of human welfare. It is a study worth pursuing partly for its intrinsic interest, but mainly because it may help us to form reasoned judgments on matters of public policy and act on them so far as our opportunities offer. Whatever exact definition of the subject we adopt, we shall be concerned not merely with money, not merely even with material objects of wealth, but with human enjoyments and satisfactions, and also with the toil and trouble which go to their making. We shall sometimes find it difficult to draw the line between what is economic and what is purely technological; and again between what is economic and what is rather political or ethical. The latter difficulty arises especially in fields in which the means to Welfare, such as Occupation and Power, have become ends of action in themselves. In dealing with it we must use our common sense as best we can.

APPENDIX TO CHAPTER I

(A) Further notes on books.

MARSHALL. *Principles of Economics*, 8th edition.
At first reading omit V, 8–11

PIGOU. *Economics of Welfare*, 4th edition.
For special attention:
Increasing and Decreasing Returns: II, 11, and App. III, 1–2
Failures of Competition: II, 9
Monopoly: II, 21–2, and App. III, 7–8
[Price Discrimination: II, 17–18]

CHAMBERLIN. *Theory of Monopolistic Competition*, 6th edition.
   At first reading, be content with summary of III and omit IX and
      Appendices
J. ROBINSON. *Economics of Imperfect Competition*.
   For special attention:
   Changes in Demand: 4
   Digression on Rent: 8
   Comparison of Monopoly and Competition: 10–14
   A World of Monopolies: 27
   [Price Discrimination: 15–16]
The references in the text to these four writers are, except when other-
wise stated, to the books here named.

(B) Articles (arranged chronologically). *E.J.* = *Economic Journal*

SRAFFA. 'The Laws of Returns under Competitive Conditions' *E.J.*
   (1926).[1]
ALLYN YOUNG. 'Increasing Returns and Economic Progress', *E.J.* (1928).
SHOVE. 'Varying Costs and Marginal Net Products', *E.J.* (1928).
—— 'Increasing Returns and the Representative Firm', *E.J.* (1930).
VINER. 'Cost Curves and Supply Curves', *Zeitschrift für National-
   ökonomie* (September 1931).[1,2]
HARROD. 'Doctrines of Imperfect Competition', *Quarterly Journal of
   Economics* (May 1934). (reprinted in *Economic Essays*).
HICKS. 'Theory of Monopoly', *Econometrica* (1935).[1]
KALDOR. 'Market Imperfection and Excess Capacity', *Economica* (1935).[1]
KAHN. 'Notes on Ideal Output', *E.J.* (1935).
HALL AND HITCH. 'Price Theory and Economic Behaviour', *Oxford
   Economic Papers* (May 1939).[3]
MACHLUP. 'Marginal Analysis and Empirical Research', *American
   Economic Review* (September 1946).
WILSON. 'Price and Outlay Policy of State Enterprise', *E.J.* (December
   1945).
ANDREWS. 'Industrial Analysis in Economics' (in *Oxford Studies in the
   Price Mechanism* (1951)).
BRUNNER. 'Competition and the Theory of the Firm', *Economia Inter-
   nazionale* (August and November 1951).

---

[1] Reprinted in American Economic Association, *Readings in Price Theory*.
[2] Reprinted in Clemence, *Readings in Economic Analysis*, Vol. II.
[3] Reprinted in *Oxford Studies in the Price Mechanism*, 1951.

EDWARDS. 'The Pricing of Manufactured Products', *Economica* (August 1952).

HARROD. 'The Theory of Imperfect Competition Revised' (in *Economic Essays* (1952)).

CHAMBERLIN. ' "Full Cost" and Monopolistic Competition', *E.J.* (June 1952).

J. ROBINSON. 'Imperfect Competition Revisited', *E.J.* (September 1953).

ROBERTSON, 'Some Recent Writings on the Theory of Pricing' (in *Economic Commentaries* (1956)).

HELP FROM THE STORY-BOOKS

How shall we approach the principles of economics? I propose to do so by adopting in succession two time-honoured and, as they may seem to you (though I hope not) childish devices. I propose first to take a lightning glance at some of the leading principles and concepts of economics at work in a setting entirely different from our own – namely, in the life of Robinson Crusoe. And I propose next to ask for the help of a visitor from another planet in elucidating the main features of the institutional framework of our own society, within which framework the main part of our study of the working of economic principles must be confined.

Let us suppose, then, that Crusoe has turned up in the traditional fashion on his island. His problem in political economy – in the management of the little State that consists of himself – is to maximise his economic welfare; our problem in economics is to observe and formulate how he does it.

(1) Let us take the story in stages. Suppose first his only need is food, and he can find one kind only, – small breadfruit growing at the top of tall trees, so that much labour is required to support life. He will soon discover two things. (i) He gets fed up with breadfruit, and ultimately sick. Some is urgently required, day by day, to stay his hunger; but after a certain point on any day each fruit yields him less and less pleasure, and after a further point any he has gathered will be left to rot. He has discovered the *law of diminishing utility*, – the larger the amount of a thing a man has, the less the satisfaction he derives from any given addition to that amount. (ii) After a point each fruit is secured at greater

inconvenience to himself. For this there are three reasons, — two inside himself and one outside. (*a*) He gets tired and inattentive, and each five minutes' labour becomes objectively less effective; but (*b*) further, each five minutes' labour becomes subjectively a greater bore; finally (*c*) he has to go farther and farther afield, or climb higher and higher trees, to get a given amount of fruit. He has discovered the *law of increasing cost*, — in the absence of any improvement in knowledge or organisation, the larger the amount of a thing produced the greater the real cost involved in making any given addition to the production. And in (*c*) he has discovered the special manifestation of the law of increasing cost known as the *law of diminishing return from land*, — an expression of the fact conditioning all our existence, that the bounty of Nature is limited, and after a point man's efforts to wring increased supplies from her become less and less effective.

If we are prepared to assume that satisfaction and its opposite are measurable things — an assumption which it would shock some of my colleagues to hear me asking you to make, and of which I shall have more to say later — we can illustrate the story so far by a simple diagram.

Along OX measure units of fruit gathered per day, along OY units of satisfaction and its opposite.
AB = curve of increments of satisfaction derived from additional fruit.
CD = curve of increments of dissatisfaction incurred on additional fruit.

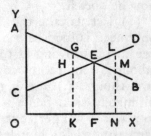

His object being to make his net balance of satisfaction as great as possible, he will stop work at the point at which extra satisfaction just balances extra dissatisfaction, i.e. will gather OF fruit per day, at which point his net balance of satisfaction is AOFE − COFE, i.e. the triangle

ACE. For this triangle is both $>$AGHC and $>$(AEC – LEM).

To fix the idea, consider how the position of the curves may change. AB will be raised throughout its length if he discovers a new and pleasanter way of cooking fruit. CD will be lowered throughout its length if he comes on a new and handy clump of trees, hitherto overlooked; or if he hits on the *labour-saving* idea of carrying fruit in his mouth or the *labour-sweetening* idea of whistling at his work (though perhaps he could hardly put both into effect simultaneously). It will be raised if he discovers among his gear some book – say Marshall's *Principles* – to the study of which he longs to return. In any of these events the position of the point of maximum satisfaction will be altered.

(2) Now suppose he is faced with a new problem. He finds a fishing-rod in his cave, and has to learn so to distribute his energies between gathering fruit and catching fish that the net total of satisfaction derived from both combined is as great as possible. This he evidently does by giving so much time per day to each occupation that the last five minutes, say, spent in each yields equal satisfaction, – otherwise he could increase his economic welfare by stopping the one a little sooner and going on with the other a little longer. He has learnt the *principle of equi-marginal return*, – that man tends to shift and adjust his resources and energies between different uses in such a way as to get the greatest total benefit from them.

Since he can now substitute some fish for the least relished part of his daily meal of fruit, he will not get tired of fruit and fish combined so easily as he did of fruit alone. Nevertheless he *will* get tired of them, – he will become aware of the *law of diminishing utility of income* or goods in general, – the greater the flow of goods and services over which a person has command, the smaller the enjoyment he derives from a given addition to that flow.

(3) Now let us face him with a fresh complication. The breadfruit season is nearly over, and he must put some aside or starve. But how much? If he is perfectly clear-sighted and firm-willed, if he thinks there is no appreciable chance either of dying or of being taken off by a passing ship, he will put aside enough to yield him a daily enjoyment throughout the winter as great as his daily enjoyment now. Note that this does not necessarily mean he will put aside enough to yield him exactly as large a daily meal in winter as he gets now; for he may foresee that his need of food will be greater, owing to the cold, or that it will be less, since he will no longer be shinning up the trees.

But being a man and not an ant, it is unlikely that he will act in just this way. This is partly a matter of calculation of chances; he may be dead in a few weeks' time, or half-way back to England, and in either case he would feel scored off if he had left a pile of uneaten fruit behind. But it is partly also, if he is a typical man, because he will find it hard to visualise effectively the intensity even of a future need which is quite certain. So for one reason and another a given increment of satisfaction today will appeal to him more strongly than the prospect of an equal increment of satisfaction three months hence, and he will probably not put by enough food to yield him a total daily enjoyment in winter as great as that which he experiences now. Thus he will be exemplifying two things, – that the principle of equi-marginal return applies as between future and present, as well as between different kinds of goods in the present; but that it applies only subject to a correction for uncertainty and to a distorting *law of overvaluation of present as compared* with future goods, – which is the economist's way of saying that most people regard a bird in the hand as worth two in the bush.

Is his store of fruit *capital*? Some would say yes, all

stored-up wealth is; others no, since it is only used to keep him alive and happy, not to aid in further production. But suppose he sits down in winter to make a new fishing-rod, his store of food clearly becomes capital, since it is being used to support him in a productive enterprise which will increase his command over Nature. But it is still *free or floating capital*, since at any moment he can change his mind and make a boat instead; when the fruit is eaten and the rod made, he has become an owner of *fixed capital*, – his savings are fixed and embodied in the rod.

But now let us vary the story, and suppose he makes the fishing-rod while the summer is still on, – not just to pass the time, but because he sees that it will increase his power to catch fish to an extent which compensates him for the loss of immediate food which results from spending part of each day in making the rod. The rod offers him sufficient *interest* to overcome his reluctance to worry about the future, and to overcome also his desire to keep plenty of spare food by him in case at any time he falls out of a breadfruit tree and breaks his leg. Thus we see interest arising from the superior effectiveness of indirect or roundabout methods of production: and whatever funny things we may hear about the rate of interest later, let us never forget how on Robinson Crusoe's island it arose.

There is no need to follow him further into the discovery of new wants and new devices. However many complications we add, we shall still see him guided by the law of diminishing utility in deciding on his ends, assisted by the principle of equi-marginal return in adapting his means to these ends, and hampered by the law of increasing cost in achieving them. We shall still see him endeavouring to distribute sensibly his time between leisure and work, his energies between different kinds of work, his income of goods between present and future, his store of capital between fixed and liquid forms, – 'sensibly' meaning in such wise as to maximise the excess of his enjoyments as consumer over the inconveniences he suffers as producer.

(4) But in conclusion we may linger a moment over these words 'consume' and 'produce'. What is to consume? Obviously not to destroy; even the fruit he does not destroy, but only rearranges internally for his own benefit (as cannibals are said to do with the souls of those whom they devour). He will consume Friday's services, when Friday comes along; and he may be said to consume the fishing-rod by holding it in use. To consume a thing, then, is to extract satisfaction from it. Similarly to produce does not mean to create, – the conjurer does not make the rabbit which he 'produces' from a hat; and what Crusoe does is to *move* things – the fruit and the fish – from a place where they are useless to a place where they will be useful, or to alter their *texture* by fire, or to alter the *shape* of a piece of wood till it becomes a fishing-rod. Indeed he may be said to be producing when he starts the day by washing his neck, though he is not turning out any material thing (except perhaps dirt as a by-product). So to produce seems to mean fundamentally to set in motion a flow of satisfaction and to consume to mean to intercept that flow for one's own ends.

In bidding farewell to Crusoe, I think we can claim these merits for him as an avenue of approach to economic theory. First, he helps us to see that the processes of balancing up and decision which it analyses are those familiar to us in the management of our individual lives. Our time and energies of body and spirit are limited, and whether we like it or not we find ourselves balancing up at the margin the most apparently incommensurable things, sport and study, friendship and foreign travel, race-going and chapel-going, in the same sort of way as Crusoe balanced fruit and fish. It is just *because* the processes are so similar that I don't think we can actually *define* economics in terms of the relation between 'ends and scarce means which have alternative uses', since that would extend its scope to the whole of human life.

Secondly, Crusoe helps us to see that these balancing problems are common to all types of economic society, from the simplest to the most complex, from the most liberal to the most controlled. The executive organs of a modern country at war do their best to behave like a myriad-headed Crusoe, balancing up at the margin the various possible uses of limited resources such as skilled labour and foreign exchange with a view to developing the maximum power to achieve victory. We may, and do, differ among ourselves as to how far it is wise or necessary to continue this, so to speak, synthetic Crusification of ourselves in times of peace, when the ultimate objective is not capable of definition with the same precision. But it is at least a gain if we can all speak more or less the same language about the nature of the problems involved.

We have, however, to examine the working of economic principles in a very different institutional set-up from that of Crusoe; and having spent half an hour in the latter's company, let us take another leaf out of the story-books, and imagine ourselves showing an intelligent visitor from another planet round our Western society, and (after explaining that we are naturally in a bit of a muddle after forty years of war and near-war) asking him to tell us what strike him as its outstanding features, – offering in turn to tell him what has been said in defence or explanation of them. I suspect he would fasten on three groups of facts, connected respectively with the concepts of Property, Economic Freedom, and the State.

I. (A) Private property itself. It is not likely he would tell us that the concept is quite unfamiliar to him, – it seems likely that there is some point at which even the Martian's spoonful of porridge becomes *his* porridge and not somebody else's. But he might tell us that on his planet property rights were confined to things destined for personal enjoyment, and that the notion of property in

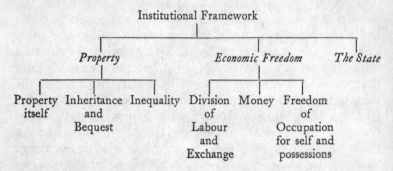

instruments of production, whether natural or man-made, was strange to him. Or again he might tell us that the Martian was allowed to own instruments in the operation of which he himself took part, but that the idea of people owning paper claims to mines and ships and machinery which they had never seen and would not know what to do with seemed to him very queer.

We should tell him that these things were much disputed among ourselves, but that running through what has been said through the ages in explanation of this institution of Property there appeared to be two main threads, — an appeal to justice and an appeal to expediency. As regards *justice*, we should say, there are probably still some people who share the somewhat extreme view once expressed by Lord Quickswood, in his little book on Conservatism, of the sanctity of the *status quo*, — 'the right of property is merely part of the right of any human being not to be gratuitously vexed by his neighbour'. In the main, however, this absolutist view chiefly survives in a pretty widespread feeling that sudden and violent interference with established rights and expectations should be avoided as far as possible, and that when it is thought necessary it should be accompanied by at any rate partial *compensation*, that is by the substitution of a more general claim on the community for any particular right, whether it be the ownership of slaves or of coal-mines, which has come to be held to be antisocial.

More commonly, we should tell our visitor, it has been felt necessary by those who defend Property on the grounds of justice to take the line that it is the just reward for Effort. In this connection we should have to tell our Martian something about the seventeenth-century philosopher John Locke and his famous argument that 'whatsoever [a man] removes out of the state that nature hath provided and left it in, he hath mixed his labour with, and joined to it something which is his own, and thereby makes it his property'. We should point out the loop-holes this argument leaves for the reply, first that not by any means everybody gets a chance to mix his labour with the soil and its products, and secondly that when, as in a modern industrial process, many hundreds of people *have* so mixed their labour, the principle doesn't go very far towards telling us who should have property in the thing and to what extent. And we should end, I think, by telling our visitor that in the main those who have been concerned to defend the institution of Property have been led or driven to fall back on its *expediency* rather than its justice. This at any rate seems to be true of two of the most powerful bodies of organised opinion who have ever influenced human affairs, – the medieval Church and the Benthamite radical utilitarian philosophers of the early nineteenth century. According to the Schoolmen, property is not a natural or divine institution, but in the degraded state of man's nature is justified as the only method of securing social peace: it must, however, be held and administered in trust for the common good. Leaping over the centuries, we come to Jeremy Bentham, who was no friend to privilege or abuse, but who held property to be necessary for the stability of society and material progress.

Within this strand of expediency we can distinguish two sub-strands: (1) the common-sense economic argument that the possession of property furnishes a powerful stimulus to work and thrift: (2) the more metaphysical argument that property is necessary for the development of personality. This has its most obvious application to personal possessions, – even a child is a poor spiritless thing unless it has some little truck or rag doll round which its personality can overflow. But it can be extended to property rights in general, because they give a man, in the old phrase, 'independence'. Indeed from this point of view the more remote their subject is from his daily work the better, – it used to be said that the Lancashire cotton operative preferred to hold shares in another cotton-mill rather than his own.

(B) So much for Property itself. But our Martian might tell us that all this was familiar to him, but that on his planet, subject to modest provision for helpless dependants, these rights lapsed at death, and that what he found strange was our laws and customs of *Inheritance and Bequest*, – the fact that property can be 'left' by will, and that even when not so 'left' it often remains private property. In reply we could tell him that we had been making big holes in this system of late years with our device of heavy death duties, though we should have to admit that as late as the late 1920s, according to an estimate then made by Josiah Wedgwood, as much as three-fifths of the private property existing in this country had been acquired by inheritance. We should explain that our laws of inheritance had commonly been defended on two different but related grounds of expediency; first, the economic one that the impulse to work and thrift is powerfully reinforced by the right to hand on the proceeds to one's children, and secondly the more broadly social one that the institution of the family thus buttressed seems to be both good in itself and useful to the survival of the race. We might, however, add that from the latter point of view the laws of most European countries, which compel equal division of a specified part of a man's property between his children, seem more logically designed than those of England, which in general permit complete freedom of bequest; and that in any event the argument is not very relevant to those cases in which there are no near relations but only what the Germans expressively call a 'laughing heir'.

(C) Finally – still under the main caption of facts connected with Property – our visitor might tell us that while Inheritance as well as Property itself was a familiar concept to him, he was amazed at the *Inequality* in which in fact on our planet these things seemed to have eventuated. We shouldn't have been able to keep from him this rough summary of Mr Campion's rough estimate[1] of the extent of this inequality in our own country in recent times. In England and Wales, 1924–30, of 22·3 million people aged twenty-five and over,

1 per cent owned more than £10,000, their property adding up to 57 per cent of the total of *c*. £14,500 million.

22 per cent owned less than £10,000, but more than £100, their property adding up to 38 per cent of the total.

77 per cent owned £100 or less, their property adding up to 5 per cent of the total.

(This somewhat overstates the inequality, for the third group includes a number of wives who were presumably enjoying the property of richer husbands.) On his planet, our Martian might tell us, property and even inheritance

---

1 See Daniel and Campion, *The Distribution of National Capital*, pp. 30 and 51. I have taken, to the nearest integer, the average of Campion's two alternative estimates. It seems likely that by 1946–7 the percentage of 'adults' owning £100 or less had, owing to the fall in the value of money, fallen to about 60, while that owning more than £10,000 was still less than 1½. (K. Langley, *Oxford Bulletin of Statistics*, December 1954, p. 355.)

had proved compatible with a much more equalitarian society, resembling apparently the 'Distributive State' of which some of our Catholic reformers have dreamed. What becomes of all the fine talk about Property and Personality, he might ask us, if in fact so few people possess any appreciable amount of it?

Well, we could, I think, point out that on our planet, in the past at all events, the amount of property would, but for this inequality in its distribution, certainly have been insufficient to fulfil the functions which it *has* fulfilled. Equality would have meant equality at a very low level; inequality has permitted, in the economic sphere, the emergence of surpluses which could be ventured in new methods of organisation and technique, thereby contributing greatly to material progress; while in the wider sphere of life and manners, from the days of Pericles to those of the Medici and onwards to our own, it has fostered the growth of art and permitted the building up and transmission of a tradition of civilised behaviour. We could assure our Martian, I think, of a pretty general agreement that by the end of the pre-1914 era inequality of possessions had become undesirably great, and of a widespread view that its further reduction is still *a* right aim, though not necessarily an overriding aim, of economic policy.[1] But on how far such inequality is itself an evil there are, I think, differences of *valuation* among us which do not turn wholly, though they do partially, on arguments of pure economics.

II. The second group of facts to which our visitor would direct our attention cluster round the concept of *Economic Freedom*. There is

(A) the basic fact of *Division of Labour and Exchange*. Some of us, he would notice, shave and make tea for

---

[1] Some of us might add that we should like to see a greater diffusion of inherited wealth encouraged by making the rate of death duty levied depend progressively on the amount *inherited* by any individual, not on the aggregate amount *left*. (See Robbins, *Lloyds Bank Review*, October 1955, pp. 13–15.)

ourselves and some do not; but at any rate we do not try to do everything for ourselves like Crusoe; nor is even the family, or the somewhat larger and looser unit the household, a nearly self-contained economic unit as it has been at some periods of our history. In the main we live by doing things for each other, and trusting that people will be pleased enough with what we do to go on keeping us alive.

We should explain to our visitor the advantages of this division of labour, — how it enables each man to make the most of his natural gifts, to keep them employed at full stretch, and to improve upon them by training and practice; and we should ask him, as I ask you, to find time to read the first three chapters of *The Wealth of Nations* (1776) in which it is explained how it is thanks above all to the division of labour that 'the accommodation of an European prince does not always so much exceed that of an industrious and frugal peasant as the accommodation of the latter exceeds that of many an African king, the absolute master of the lives and liberties of ten thousand naked savages'. Our visitor might be much impressed; or he might on the other hand reply that on his planet they had been trying for a long time to limit the division of labour as much as they could possibly afford to do, partly on the ground that they had found that it had landed many worthy Martians in situations where their special skill was a drug in the market, and partly because they thought that versatility and variety of occupation were highly desirable things in themselves.

Next in this group we come to (B) the fact that we do not as a rule exchange things with one another directly, but through the agency of tickets called *Money*. This is a very great convenience; but it has its disadvantages, since it is open to people to accumulate these tickets for a time, and then to release their accumulations, in both cases with disturbing effects on their neighbours. Our Martian might tell us that his people were still living in a régime of barter; or on the other hand that they had discovered a monetary system which worked with perfect smoothness, and avoided our unhappy alternations of excessive and deficient monetary demand.

(C) There is finally the fact that normally our arrangements accord to the individual legal *Freedom of Occupation* for himself and his possessions, carrying with it the right to make binding contracts. This is not a necessary accompaniment, our Martian might remind us, of the division of labour. There might be on his planet, as there was on ours to some extent in the Middle Ages and tends to be again in time of war, a highly differentiated economy practising exchange and using money, in which nevertheless the function of the individual is determined by fiat or custom rather than by free choice. The assumptions lying at the back of the system of economic freedom have been expressed — indeed over-expressed — in two passages of Adam Smith's *Wealth of Nations* so famous and eloquent that we should insist on reading them aloud to our visitor. 'The property which every man has in his own labour, as it is the original foundation of all other property, so it is the most sacred and inviolable. The patrimony of a poor man lies in the strength and dexterity of his hands; and to hinder him from employing this strength and dexterity in what manner he thinks proper without injury to his neighbour, is a plain violation of this most sacred property' (I, 10). 'Every individual is continually exerting himself to find out the most advantageous employment for whatever capital he can command. It is his own advantage indeed and not that of the society which he has in view. But the study of his own advantage naturally, or rather necessarily, leads him to prefer that employment which is most advantageous to society' (IV, 2). Economic freedom, that is to say, is to be justified on grounds both of natural right and of expediency. But even Adam Smith knew well enough that in this second passage he was pitching it a bit high; and most modern champions of economic freedom would perhaps put the whole thing less flamboyantly, and say rather that in a world where the future is always highly uncertain and obscure, there is prima facie great advantage in having responsibility for the use of resources dispersed and decentralised as widely as possible, on the ground that out of the welter of individual judgments a more satisfactory result is likely to emerge than could ever be achieved in practice by a single all-directing will.

It is moreover evident, as our Martian would tell us after he had poked about a bit, that economic freedom does not exist as fully in fact as it does in law. It is often limited in practice by those already engaged in some trade or occupation, – by a giant combine which can use its strength to ruin any outsider who dares to set up in competition, by a trade union which limits entry to a trade by apprenticeship rules or by conventions, e.g. about what work is and what is not to be regarded as suitable for women. It is limited further by inequalities of education and opportunity bound up with the systems of property and inheritance. An agricultural labourer is legally free to become a barrister or a stockbroker: but what, our Martian might ask, is the use of that? All we could tell him in reply, but it is a good deal, is that under modern educational policies inequality of *opportunity* is being modified a good deal more rapidly than inequality of *wealth*.

Our visitor would not have failed to observe that men use their economic freedom, such as in each case it is, and their rights of contract, in three different ways: (1) to *compete* with one another; (2) to *co-operate* with those producing some different service from themselves; (3) to *combine* with those performing the same sort of service as themselves. And we could tell him that we find that this triple relationship of competition, co-operation or complementarity, and combination gives rise to many of the most difficult problems, both theoretical and practical, of terrestrial economics, such as the relation between capital in general and labour in general, the relation between skilled and unskilled labour, the relation between British industry and the industry of Germany or India.

III. *The State*. Finally our Martian would tell us that he had observed that we did not appear to believe that economic freedom, even when realised, always produced the best results, since we maintained in existence a monster called *the State*, whose functions appeared to be not only to preserve and protect the institutions of property and economic freedom, but also to limit them in particular cases by preventing people from doing this or that (such as selling themselves into slavery or erecting buildings more than a certain number of feet high), and again to clear up the mess when the operation of these principles led to the shipwreck of individual lives. He would probably tell us, and I dare say we should agree, that we, that is, the members of Western nations taken as a whole, did not seem to have quite made up our minds whether we regarded the functions of the State as consisting mainly in police and salvage action of these kinds, or whether we thought that it should also perform a number of positive functions of a kind which private enterprise is likely to neglect, or to perform badly, or whether finally we held that it should go farther still and, in the words of one of our best English journalists, 'assume responsibility for the purposive direction of the economic and social climate in which the community lives'. We should probably warn him that on this question of the rôle of the State he would find a somewhat different smell in the air on the two sides of the Atlantic Ocean; and that, coming down to details, he would find that in some countries certain branches of economic activity were now monopolised by the State, while in others they were still open to individual enterprise.

He for his part *might* be able to tell us of some quite different arrangement on his own planet. He might tell us that Martians really did practise economic freedom to the limit and were a perfectly contented community of logical anarchists. Or he might tell us that they had a single centralised authority for the whole planet; or again that while authority was decentralised and devolved, the devolution was not on geographical but on functional lines, rules for the government of economic life being made by occupational syndicates entering into treaty relations with one another. In any of these events our Nation-State, aiming with greater or less directness at promoting the welfare of its own people and often colliding with other Nation-States in the process, might seem a queer affair to him. And we might perhaps reply that it sometimes seems a bit odd to us too, and that we have been making all sorts of fumbling experiments at wider groupings and at blurring the edges of national sovereignty; but that somehow or other, when it comes to the point, the concept of the Nation-State, which it has taken so many centuries to distil in the cauldron of history, seems to have set and crystallised uncommon hard.

III

THE NATIONAL INCOME

Living within the framework of institutions which we have discussed, the residents in any territory come into possession of an annual *income* of goods and services. It seems inevitable, both statistically and politically, that those of us who are lucky enough to have one should take the *nation* as our unit for purposes of study, – which doesn't prejudge the question of whether we should regard it as of unique importance for purposes of policy. The national income has increasingly become the focal point of economic analysis, and also – quite rightly – the object of a great display of statistical virtuosity; and I must simplify drastically if we are not to be held up more than is expedient, and must concentrate on concepts and principles, rather than methods or actual figures. Nevertheless here (Table, section (1)) *are* some figures from the official Blue-book, arranged after my own fashion, which we will run through presently.

The national income consists, predominantly at least, of goods and services, but to be manageable in discourse its magnitude must be expressed in a common measure, namely money. In evaluating this money sum, we must keep in mind the purpose we want it to serve. From my present point of view, we want it to be as nearly as possible usable as an indicator (i) of changes in the economic welfare of a nation between one time and another, (ii) of differences in economic welfare between one nation and another (to simplify exposition, I shall talk almost entirely in terms of the former comparison). But whatever our purpose, we must have regard to common sense and the nature of our material. My discussion thus falls into four parts:

(I) How shall we build up our figure for a year Y?

(II) How shall we treat this figure to make it comparable with a similarly built figure for year X?

(III) How far is the figure so treated really a good indicator of changes in economic welfare?

(IV) How must we adjust the figure so as to make it usable for certain other purposes?

I

(see Table, section (2))

A. The method which arises most clearly from our conception of the national income, and which should presumably be followed if the material permits, consists of four stages.[1]

(1) Estimate the 'net product' of each branch of industrial activity, including agriculture, industry proper, merchanting, transport. In the case of each industry, this means taking the selling value of its output, and deducting the cost of materials, fuel, etc., bought from other industries. In the case of merchanting it means making a direct estimate of the gross margin between what the merchant sells goods at and what he pays for them, and in the case of transport making a direct estimate of gross receipts; and then in each case deducting the cost of fuel etc. bought from other industries. The potential selling value of produce consumed by the producer should be included so far as possible when it is important, as of course it is, especially in a peasant economy.

[1] [A critic points out that apparently I did not even mention the alternative procedure of aggregating the expenditures of various categories of domestic buyers of final output and then doctoring for foreign trade. This, I am afraid, is true; but for my purposes what I called Method A, which I think was first laid out in the *Report of the First Census of Production* (Cd. 6320 of 1912 – see the summary by Bowley in *The Division of the Product of Industry*, p. 59) seemed sufficient and more fundamental. My class were receiving instruction at other hands in the mystiques of the Official Bluebook (including, no doubt, the justification for describing, in Table I, *foreigners'* expenditure on *British* goods as part of *British* 'national expenditure'!)].

(2) Deduct the value of the goods needed for keeping capital intact. This is a highly tricky and ambiguous conception, about which much has been written, and which we must not allow to detain us. But it is clear that such goods do not really form part of income; though it is of high importance that in emergency the resources normally devoted to making them can be diverted to the purpose of adding to the flow of goods available for immediate consumption.

(3) Add the value of extra-industrial services of all kinds, – domestics, dons, actors, soldiers, M.P.s; also the services of property hired for direct enjoyment, i.e. primarily of houses. Note that (i) we include services purchased by Government on the ground that the public, which is the ultimate consumer, must be held to desire them. We ought strictly to exclude those services, e.g. of many Board of Trade officials, which are in the nature of a business expense paid for collectively and are thus already reflected in the value of industrial output; but this is usually judged to be in practice an impossible refinement. (ii) On practicability grounds, we exclude the enormously important unpaid services rendered by women in homes, – though this may be an appreciable source of comparative error, especially as between war and peace conditions. (iii) We include the services of houses lived in by their owners, but do not attempt to extend this principle to cars, furniture, etc.

(4) Correct the total so reached for external transactions, i.e. (i) deduct exports and add, at their value to the consumer, imports of goods and services, (ii) deduct increments of foreigners' claims on us or add increments of our claims on foreigners, – our true income is by so much less in the first case, greater in the second, than the flow of goods and services becoming available to us in the period. *Gifts* from abroad, e.g. Marshall Aid, should also be deducted to reach true 'income'. And there is one more

correction to be made, which I will tell you about later.
B. In principle we can reach the same result by summing
the recorded money incomes of the members of the
nation, including companies, public corporations (i.e. the
nationalised industries), and Governments (Central and
Local) *qua* property-owners, provided the total so
obtained is doctored in the following ways.

(1) As in method A, we must add the value of produce
consumed by the growers, – though not the value of
houses lived in by the owners, since that is supposed to be
looked after in recorded money income. So, in principle,
is the deduction for upkeep of capital, since profits are
calculated after allowance for depreciation, though difficulties may arise here through differences between the
true amounts and those conventionally allowed.

(2) We must deduct incomes which are mere transfers,
notably interest on the dead-weight national debt and
old-age and unemployment allowances etc.

(3) We must add indirect taxes on goods and services
(including the use of houses and other buildings), home-
produced or imported, since these have found their way
into the selling value of product under Method A, but
not into the total of incomes under Method B. To be
logical we must correspondingly deduct the subsidies
given to certain branches of production, though this lands
us in a paradox which to my mind has been insufficiently
appreciated, viz. that when services are rendered *wholly*
free to the public – e.g. those of policemen – they are
counted in at cost, while when they are rendered *partly*
free – e.g. the provision of privately produced milk or
eggs at less than cost price – they are counted at what the
consumer pays for them.

Note that no correction is required for external transactions. The income received from exports and from the
ownership of claims on foreigners, which appears in
Method B, must be equal to the untaxed value of imports

plus the increase (positive or negative) in claims on foreigners which appear in Method A.

Note further that the two methods are only alternative over *part* of the route; for extra-industrial services they are identical, – there is no measure of the 'product' of the Prime Minister except what he is in fact paid.

II

In order to compare the figure thus reached for year Y with a figure reached by similar methods for year X, we must correct the former as best we can for the change in the purchasing power of money. Now there is no unequivocal measure of this: the money cost of the collection of things composing real income in Y may have moved, between X and Y, in a different proportion, or even in a different direction, from the money cost of the collection of things composing real income in X. Let us write L for the ratio $\dfrac{\text{price of X-income at Y,}}{\text{price of X-income at X}}$ and P for the ratio $\dfrac{\text{price of Y-income at Y}}{\text{price of Y-income at X}}$. Normally P will be less than L; for people will have so adjusted their purchases as to buy more, at Y than at X, of the things which have risen least or fallen most in price, and less of those which have risen most or fallen least. The initials stand for Paasche and Laspeyre, – two gentlemen about whom I am afraid I can tell you nothing.

If we knew these two ratios L and P, which of course would involve knowing the quantity and price of each several item for both years, and if we took some mix-up of them – $\sqrt{LP}$ is that most favoured by some of the pundits – we should have done very well indeed; though even so the result would not necessarily be very significant for economic welfare if tastes have changed greatly. In practice we shall have to do something much rougher, namely use a ratio showing the change in cost of some collection of things narrower than the whole national income, and relevant only to one – or perhaps indeed not to either – of the two years. Dividing the Y money income figure by this, we get the best we can do for a single figure for Y to compare with the undoctored figure for X in order to show the change in real income.

III

The figure so obtained is an index of 'real income', i.e. of a sum of objective flows of goods and services, and we have seen that even as this it has a good many shortcomings. But it has still further shortcomings as an index of what has happened to economic welfare.

(1) The quantity of satisfaction yielded by a given objective flow depends on the distribution of the flow as well as on its size; it is possible for instance that economic welfare might be increased if the distribution of the flow became more equal even though its total fell.

(2) Real income is an index of gross satisfaction, not of net satisfaction, and thus takes no account of such changes in dissatisfaction as may be brought about by, for instance, a lengthening or shortening of the hours of labour.

(3) Equally it takes no account of the dissatisfaction of non-work. We have seen that *total* welfare may be greater if a given income is earned by ten people than if it is earned by nine, one standing involuntarily idle, even though the idle man is given an equal share; though we found it difficult to decide whether this is or is not an *economic* consideration.

(4) By including the output of *all* industries and Government purchases of *all* services, we have – as fore-shadowed in an earlier lecture – treated Power *as if* it were Welfare. But if we do this, our figure, in time of war or near-war, at least needs a footnote to indicate that the

composition of the real national income has become somewhat odd.[1] And the same perhaps is true in peace if half the population are engaged in spying on, or even in issuing orders to, the other half.

(5) Finally, even if interpreted very widely, 'economic welfare', as we have defined it, still does not tell the whole tale. It is an aggregate, and it is a flow during a given limited period. Hence two consequences follow:

(i) We may well want a second set of figures telling the story of real income *per head*, which for some purposes, though not for all, may be the more interesting conception.

(ii) For the purpose of throwing light on the whole economic outlook for one nation as compared with others, we may want a further footnote on the *durability* of its sources of income. Does this come largely from mines which will soon peter out, – a fact impossible to do full justice to in the deductions we have made for depreciation? Or does much of it come from nascent industries, likely to grow in strength and cohesion? Our footnote may easily reach considerable length!

IV

We have reached the border-line of our last theme. For what other purposes than as an index of changes in economic welfare may we need a figure of the national income, and what changes does our figure require in order to adapt it to these other purposes?

(1) If we want an index of *productive power* rather than of welfare, it is better to take off the indirect taxes and add in the subsidies, thus reaching what has come to be known as the 'net national income at factor cost'. This is now probably the best-known concept of national income,

---

[1] Mr Reddaway once described the element of arms expenditures in the national income as 'regrettable necessities'. The element of arms expenditures in the national income of a potential enemy should presumably be described as 'unnecessary regrettabilities'.

though it is not the one from which I have chosen to start.

(2) In order to study the *distribution* of income between factors of production and between income-classes, we must first deduct Government income from property etc. and add the 'transfer' incomes. We can then go on to see how this new total is divided up (*a*) as it stands and (*b*) after allowance has been made for the payment of direct and indirect taxes on the one hand, and for the enjoyment of services rendered free or below cost on the other. This last process of correction involves a considerable arbitrary element when we come to allocate the benefits of defence, justice and so forth.

(3) Of all the ways in which the *composition* of the national income can be analysed, one is of unique interest, namely the division into (*a*) things being currently enjoyed, (*b*) net additions to capital wealth. The latter element in turn consists of two parts, (i) additions to working capital, – goods in process or in store, (ii) additions to fixed capital, – buildings, machinery, etc. As regards (i), I must now disclose that, if prices are rising or falling *during* the year under ex~ ..ination, our figure, by whichever method calculated, will be too large or too small, as the case may be. For it will contain, as a positive or negative element, not merely, as it should do, the money value of the increment of goods in store or process, but also, as it should *not* do, the increment in the money value of an unchanged quantity of such goods. This results from the way in which output and profits are habitually reckoned, and has been the source of much difficulty in estimating the true national income in some recent years.

As regards (ii), net additions to fixed capital, it is very difficult, as I have already hinted, especially if prices have been changing rapidly over recent years, to calculate the correct figure to deduct from the *gross* output of fixed capital goods for 'goods needed to keep fixed capital intact'. The official Blue-book now does give us such a figure, with many warnings that we use it at our own peril, as I have done in the table, section (1): it still does not embody it in its own main table, but we can no longer make the old joke that the one figure which you will not find in the National Income Blue-book is a figure of the national income. Section (3) of my table is just a little exercise wherewith to remind oneself that a country in which some obviously new, and apparently additional, capital instruments are coming to birth may nevertheless be consuming more than its true income.

But what all this leads up to in the present connection is that, even if we think we have got a firm figure for the net national income, it may be not this figure, but that of the *gross* income, including *all* new capital goods, which is really the more significant for certain purposes, for instance for following the course of fluctuations in industrial activity and employment.

TABLE (2)

(1)

UNITED KINGDOM NATIONAL INCOME[1]

	1938	1951	1955
		£ million	
Apparent gross national product at market prices	5,680	15,347	19,258
Less stock appreciation	+80	−750	−200
True gross national product at market prices	5,760	14,597	19,058
Less depreciation	−359	−1,163	−1,558
National income at market prices ...	5,401	13,434	17,500
Less indirect taxes	−622	−2,272	−2,620
Add subsidies	57	468	346
National income at factor cost ...	4,816	11,630	15,226
Residual error	−	−25	32
Less net income from Government property	−28	+38	−79
Less income of public corporations ...	+4	+133	+128
Add interest on national debt ...	213	550	707
Add social security etc. payments ...	275	784	1,115
Private income	5,280	13,110	17,129
Less company income	−278	−1,487	−1,772
Personal income	5,002	11,623	15,357
Less social security etc. payments ...	−275	−784	−1,115
Personal income from work and property	4,727	10,839	14,242

[1] Note on reading the main table. A minus sign means 'subtract'. When the figure to be subtracted is itself negative, as notably in the case of the true income of the public corporations, attention is called to the fact by inserting a plus sign.

		Distribution of					
		Stock Appreciation			*Depreciation*		
		1938	1951	1955	1938	1951	1955
Government ...	...	−	93	14	85	255	326
Public corporations	...	−	80	18	8	229	306
Companies ...	...	−60	465	122	176	373	566
Persons ...	...	−20	112	46	90	306	360
Total ...	...	−80	750	200	359	1,163	1,558
of which houses	...	...	...	...	54	212	254

	Index (original base 1948) *of*					
	Price			*Quantity*		
	1938	1951	1955	1938	1951	1955
Consumers' expenditure	100	225	255	100	103	115
Net fixed investment ...	100	279	321	100	88	137

(2)

Method A	*Method B*
Net output of industries etc.	Money incomes
+ self-consumed produce	+ self-consumed produce
− depreciation	− transfers
+ services	+ indirect taxes
+ annual value of houses	− subsidies
+ imports cum tax	
+ imports of 'securities'	
− exports	

(3)

P = gross product
Y = income
C = consumption
A_1 = addition to working capital
A_2 = addition to fixed capital
D = depreciation (needed replacements)
M = actual replacements
N = new constructions

$$Y = C + A_1 + A_2$$
$$= C + A_1 + M + N - D$$
$$P = Y + D$$
$$= C + A_1 + M + N$$

If M is less than D, A_2 is less than N.

If $(M + N + A_1)$ is less than D, Y is less than C.

INTRODUCTION TO THE THEORY OF VALUE

THE THEORY OF DEMAND

We have our concept of the National Income: what shall we do with it? The natural thing might seem to be to examine directly the causes determining its *size*. This evidently depends primarily on the quantity and quality of the nation's productive resources, – its inheritance of soil and climate, its equipment of buildings and instruments, the numbers and quality of its people; secondarily on the degree of fullness with which these resources are being utilised. If this were a general course on the economic condition of the United Kingdom I should proceed directly to study these matters; but in a course on 'Principles', supplemented in your pabulum by others, a different procedure is more convenient. We don't want to get bogged down in physical geography, engineering technique or educational policy; nor to get involved *prematurely* in difficult problems connected with fluctuations of economic activity. I shall therefore proceed by examining the forces determining the *composition* of the national income; and I shall do this by building up a *theory of value*, which will be found to throw light on other problems also. I shall not lay down any very rigid assumptions; but in the main, for a good many weeks, we shall be examining the forces determining the way the national income is made up in a country of which the following things can be said. First, that it is living under a régime which is basically one of economic freedom, but is tempered by the intervention of the State. Secondly, that it is self-contained, i.e. we ignore the complications connected with dealings with foreigners. Thirdly, that in it resources are fairly fully and continuously (which does not mean 100 per cent) employed; and fourthly (which may or may not be the same thing, – we won't prejudge the question) that money is in some sense playing a neutral part, acting as a lubricant to the whole system, but not introducing any distortions into it. We shall follow English tradition in not attempting to attain a still greater degree of logical precision by assuming at the start that our system is a completely *static* one; i.e. we shall take account in our analysis, as best we can, (i) of the phenomena of *growth* and *progress*, (ii) of the fact that even in a community which as a whole is displaying steady growth, the business life of the individual is conducted in a mist of *uncertainty* about the results of his own and other people's actions.

On these assumptions, we proceed, as stated, by building up a theory of value. What is this, and why is it important? The value of one thing in terms of another is the amount of the second thing which will be given or obtained for a unit of the first, e.g. the number of pounds of butter which can be exchanged for a ton of coal. The value of a thing in terms of money is called its price; and for the present – though we may see reason to depart from this – we can interpret our condition that money is behaving 'neutrally' as meaning that we can regard the price of a thing as measuring its value in terms of things in general, so that the concepts of value and price are interchangeable. A theory of value, then, is an attempt to explain the forces determining the value of one thing in terms of other things, – assumed for our purposes to be identical with its value in terms of money.

The primary reason, in my view, for the central importance assigned to the theory of value in economic study is that until it is cleared up the connection between the ordinary market processes which we observe and the economic welfare whose promotion is the object of our study must remain obscure. A more obvious (and perhaps more generally accepted) reason is that already hinted, – namely that a theory of the relative value of different goods is also *ipso facto* a theory of their relative scales of output, that is, of the way in which the national income is made up and the nation's productive forces distributed between various uses and occupations. Goods and services go about the place bearing, figuratively at least, a label stating their value, which acts as a signal both to producers and consumers. If the price of a thing goes up, that is a warning to consumers to restrict consumption, a stimulus to producers to expand production; if it goes down, that is an encouragement to consumers, a deterrent to producers. Value, then, is the barrier which limits consumption, the finger-post which guides production. It has a power over economic life comparable to that of an ancient emperor or modern commissar; no wonder that its study is important.

But there is a further point. Not only do finished goods bear their label, but also the services of each one of us and our possessions. The theory of value can be extended to the 'factors of production' and includes a 'theory of distribution', i.e. of the forces determining the distribution of the national income among the renderers of different kinds of services and the owners of different kinds of resources. The theories of rent, profit, interest and wages are special cases, each with its own peculiar modifications, of the general theory of value. So is the theory of the value of money, with all its implications for the study of the fluctuations and flaggings of general activity and employment. These huge ramifications of the theory of value constitute a further reason why the serious student of economics should not grudge the time and mental discipline demanded of him in studying its foundations.

Let us begin with a humdrum statement: 'the value of a thing in a market depends on demand and supply'. (i) What is a thing? We use the word here to mean a *class* of individual objects, and to indicate this sometimes use the cumbrous word 'commodity'. How widely or narrowly we draw the boundaries of the class is an arbitrary matter, depending on convenience: e.g. for some purposes each separate kind or grade of tea is best regarded as a separate commodity, for other purposes tea, coffee and cocoa can all be regarded as forming part of the commodity composed of substances which, when infused with hot water, form acceptable breakfast drinks. (ii) What is a market? Not necessarily a definite area, but 'any set of conditions in which buyers and sellers are in such close touch with one another that the prices of similar articles tend easily and quickly to equality' (Cournot). But market-hood, like thing-hood, is a matter of degree. There is thus an infinite gradation between the sale of rugs in an Eastern bazaar, where a separate 'market' is called into existence for every transaction, and the sale of wheat or cotton of a given grade at prices determined in a world market. We shall later be concerned a good deal with imperfect markets; we start by looking at the determination of value in a perfect market. (iii) 'Depends on demand and supply' – that looks an easy saying and is a hard one, which will occupy us for a long time to come. Let us begin by building up a *theory of demand*.

THE THEORY OF DEMAND

In view of unsettled controversies, it will be well to start our analysis of demand from as objective an angle as possible. We thus lay down, as generalisations based on observation, the two companion propositions:

(i) Other things equal, the more a man has of a thing, the smaller the price he will be prepared to pay for an additional unit of it;

(ii) Other things equal, the lower the price at which a thing is offered, the more of it a man will be prepared to buy.

These propositions apply both to *stocks* of a thing and, more importantly, to weekly or annual rates of purchase. (I need hardly say that man includes woman, the shopping housewife being indeed the heroine of this part of the economic story.)

It is evident that in these statements the phrase 'other things equal' is bearing a heavy load, in other words that, if we had omitted it, we should have had to point out that our empirical 'law of demand' is subject to numerous and formidable exceptions. Concentrating on version (ii), we shall sometimes observe an increase in a man's purchases of a thing to be associated with a *rise* in its price. Most of the reasons for this can be subsumed under four headings.

(1) The influence of *expected further changes* in price in the same direction. If a price rises, people sometimes rush in to buy for fear of missing the bus, or in the hopes of reselling at a profit; if it falls, they sometimes hold off in hopes of a further fall, or in fear of being left with the baby. This applies to some extent to the more durable of those consumption goods with which we are at present concerned, e.g. clothes or cars. But it is of much more importance in connection with staple goods at wholesale, securities, etc.; and we can conveniently postpone its further study till we come to the study of fluctuations in the general purchasing power of money and in economic activity.

(2) A change in *taste or state of need* on the part of the purchaser. A rise in the price of sugar will not deter him from increasing his purchases if, as a result of the prohibition of alcohol, he has developed a taste for sweets; nor will a further rise in the price of clothes if, as the result of previous rises, he has deferred replacement purchases

so long that he can defer them no longer, – he has in effect become a different man.

(3) A change in the purchaser's *income*, overbearing the effect of the change in price. Here the story gets a little bit complicated. If a man's income is unchanged, a rise in the price of meat will probably cause him to reduce his consumption of meat; but if his income simultaneously rises, his consumption of meat may well increase in spite of the rise in price. Again, if a man's income is unchanged, a fall in the price of margarine will probably induce him to expand his consumption; but if his income simultaneously increases, his consumption of margarine may well *decrease* in spite of the fall in price, because he will now be in a position to buy butter instead of margarine. Thus in both instances the effect of the rise in income pulls against the effect of the change in price, in the meat case making him buy more in spite of a rise in price, in the margarine case making him buy less in spite of a fall in price. But the reason why income pulls against price is different in the two cases. In the meat case it is because the thing is one of which, its price remaining unchanged, he would naturally buy more when his income increases; in the margarine case, it is because the thing is one of which in similar circumstances he would naturally buy less. Things of this latter class are sometimes called 'inferior goods', and we shall meet them again.

(4) Changes in the price of *related goods*, whether the relation be one of rivalry or of what is called complementarity. A fall in the price of tea may be associated with diminished consumption if accompanied by a still greater fall in the price of coffee; a fall in the price of soda-water may be associated with diminished consumption if accompanied by a sufficient *rise* in the price of whisky. Except for a small knot of complements, all or most things are *to some extent* rivals to any one particular

thing as candidates for the consumer's choice, even if they apparently fill very different needs; but of course in some cases the relationship of rivalry or substitutability is particularly close.

Thus in formal language the amount of a thing demanded by a man is a function not merely of its price but of a great many other things, notably his income and the prices of 'related' goods. If we allow ourselves to draw up a demand schedule exhibiting the quantities he will buy at various prices, we must realise that its validity depends on the assumption not merely that the other determinants do not change as the price alters, but that each of them has, in the mathematical sense, a particular value, e.g. that his income is £500 a year, not £1,000 or £250.

Subject to this caution, there is much convenience in using such a schedule as a tool of analysis, and in speaking of it as *being* the man's 'demand' or 'the state of his demand' for the thing in question, reserving the terms an 'increase' or 'decrease in his demand' to denote a raising or lowering of the whole schedule due to changes in one or other of the other determinants. Such a schedule can of course, if we allow ourselves to smooth out discontinuities and roughnesses, be represented geometrically by a curve.

Isolating the effect of a fall in price in this way, can we now say unequivocally that it will always be in the direction of increasing consumption of the thing in question? Not with certainty even now, for this reason. The effect of a fall in the price of A is twofold, – to increase the attractiveness of A to the purchaser relatively to other things, and to increase the purchasing power of his money income. Generally speaking we can neglect this latter effect; but not if A is both (1) an 'inferior good' on which he would naturally spend less if his money income were to increase, (2) a thing on which he has

E

been spending a large proportion of his money income, so that the potential release of purchasing power due to the fall in its price is equivalent to an appreciable increase of money income. In such a case he may actually buy less of the thing in consequence of a fall in price and more in consequence of a rise; and it has often been asserted that this is the case with the demand of very poor families for bread.

But normally the limiting case may be taken to be that in which consumption is unaffected by a rise or fall in price, and in which the 'elasticity of demand' is said to be zero. On this concept of the elasticity of demand I have nothing to add to what is said in the books, and will only remind you of the following points.

(1) A precise definition can only be given in symbols, but a good verbal approximation is that the elasticity of a man's demand for a thing is the ratio of the percentage increase in his consumption to the percentage fall in price by which it is induced, both being assumed small. The mathematician naturally thinks of this elasticity as a negative expression, but in ordinary discourse it is more convenient to treat it as a positive one, so that one can speak of one elasticity being greater than another without ambiguity.

(2) Broadly speaking, elasticity of demand is small in the case of necessaries or of things which the consumer insists on treating as such, such as tobacco; and in the case of things which at most absorb only a small part of income. It is great for comforts, for things which have a large number of uses of various degrees of urgency, for things for which it is reasonably easy to find substitutes.

(3) Even when we are dealing with a demand schedule in the sense explained, i.e. isolating the effect of price changes on quantity demanded, we must be taken to be making some assumption about the *time* we are allowing for the effect of the price-change to show itself. Generally

speaking, the longer the interval, the greater the elasticity of demand, since the consumer will have had more time to adapt his habits to the change, – for instance by installing new gear to take advantage of a fall in the price of electricity.

(4) The concepts of demand schedule and elasticity of demand can of course be extended from an individual purchaser to a whole market, – indeed they work better for a whole market, for individual gaps and roughnesses get smoothed out. A fall of 10 per cent in price will not induce Brown to buy a second wedding-cake, but may well induce Jones to buy one when he otherwise wouldn't have; generally speaking every fall in price brings a thing within range of a new group of consumers.

It remains to say a little – I am not equipped to say more – about the attempts which have been made to distil theoretical demand schedules of the type described out of the material afforded by the available statistics of prices and consumption. These attempts fall into two main classes. In one we take the recorded figures of price and consumption of some commodity in successive years; we attempt to eliminate obvious disturbing influences such as growth of population and changes in the general value of money and we then experiment, using various statistical techniques, in order to see what assumptions about the relative strength of the remaining influences – mainly relative price on the one hand and changing real income per head and tastes on the other – best fit the facts. The pioneer Schultz, working on these lines, concluded that the elasticity of demand for sugar in the United States remained pretty steady at about 0·5 or 0·4 in the fifty-five years ending 1929, but that while in the first two (twenty year) sub-periods of this period the demand schedule shifted upwards at an annual rate of about $1\frac{1}{2}$ per cent and $1\frac{1}{4}$ per cent respectively, in the last (fifteen year) sub-period the growth had ceased, – an interesting conclusion. The elasticities of demand for all the ten crops studied by Schultz worked out well below 1·0, that for wheat in the inter-war years being as low as 0·2. In an important article in the *Statistical Journal*, 1945, Stone, working on a somewhat similar method, also found elasticities of demand of less than 1, though in some cases not much less, for a number of things of common consumption – beer, tobacco, soap, telegrams – in this country in the inter-war period, though for certain kinds of household equipment in the United States – refrigerators etc. – he found an elasticity markedly greater than one.

In the massive volume, *The Measurement of Consumers' Expenditure and Behaviour in the United Kingdom* 1920–1938, published in 1954, Stone with his collaborators has revised and greatly extended his earlier work. Most of the elasticities still come out less than 1; it is to be noted that they are all very short-period ones, since he uses annual data and compares price and consumption in the same year. Apparently there are technical difficulties about working with a substantially longer assumed lag between price-change and effect on consumption; but, though I am not really competent to criticise, I cannot help suspecting that in avoiding these difficulties the influence of price on consumption has been under-estimated, – as has been shown to be the case with some of the estimates which have been made of elasticities of demand in international trade.

The other class of attempts uses the information collected in family budgets to study the relative amounts of a given thing consumed at a given date by persons whose incomes differ, but not so widely as to make it unreasonable to assume that they have similar tastes, and so, from the way different people behave, to infer how the *same* people would behave if their incomes were increased or diminished. What this method yields directly is the *income elasticity* of demand, defined as the ratio of the proportionate change in consumption to the proportionate change in income which induces it, both changes being assumed small. With the growing interest in fluctuations of income, this concept has become increasingly widely used in recent years. To the best of my understanding – which, however, in these regions is apt to flicker somewhat – from the income elasticities of demand for various things, as obtained from comparison of family budgets, it is not possible to derive with confidence the absolute values of the price elasticities of demand for the several things; but it might be possible,[1] on certain reasonable assumptions, to get an idea of their *relative* magnitudes, so that if we could ascertain one of them by a more direct method we could go on to fix the others. In any case, if the influence of *income* on the consumption of any commodity can be ascertained by this budget method, this lightens the task of isolating the influence of *price* by the time-series method; and Stone, in the volume just mentioned, has used the two methods in conjunction in this manner.

[1] Pigou, *Economics of Welfare*, Appendix II.

V

DEMAND AND UTILITY

I have so far, in deference to modern fashion, presented the theory of demand in as objective and behaviouristic a manner as possible, though I fear the fact that we are dealing with humans, not atoms or even ants, has sometimes peeped through. But we must now face the question, what is the relation between the empirical law of demand and that utility or satisfaction which we found to be the ultimate object of economic study? I will first present what I *believe* to be the Marshallian view, though I cannot guarantee that if we could have the old gentleman in the room with us he would not repudiate me, and I will then say something about the grounds on which this view has been criticised and alternative treatment proposed.

On the Marshallian view, as I understand it, there is nothing inherently absurd about supposing that utility or satisfaction is a quantitative and 'measurable' entity, in the sense that additional lumps of it can be directly compared with one another in respect of size by the person who experiences them. Hence it is reasonable to suppose that behind the observational law of demand – 'the more a man has of a thing, the less he will be prepared to pay, other things being equal, for an additional unit' – there lies a psychological law of diminishing utility – 'the more a man has of a thing, the less the utility he derives from an additional unit of it'. Indeed it is arguable that this law, being based on *introspection* – on what we know of our own minds – is really more firmly established than the observational law of demand, which as we have seen has to be extracted with some difficulty from the welter of recorded statistics.

Let us call the utility of that unit of a thing which a

man is just induced to buy, its marginal utility to him. The fact that utility is measurable, in the sense indicated, does not mean that we, as observers, could ever measure directly this marginal utility, in the way that we could measure the length of a man's nose. But it does mean that, on the assumption that he is behaving rationally, we can take the price per unit which he is paying for each thing as an indirect measure of its marginal utility to him. For on this assumption of rational behaviour he will be so distributing his expenditure between different things that the utility received in return for the last pound spent in each several direction is equal, so that he could not gain any extra utility by transferring a pound from one direction of expenditure to another.

Let us pause for a moment to look at this assumption of rational behaviour. From the fact that a man acts in a certain way all that we can directly infer is that he is impelled by some desire to act in that way. Our money measure therefore, such as it is, is primarily a measure of *desire*. To use it as a measure of *utility* we have to assume first that our man's desire for different things is proportionate to the utility which he expects to get from them, and secondly that the utility which he does get is equal to the utility which he expects to get. I will return to the question of the validity of these assumptions later; for the moment I continue to make them. The point we have reached, then, is that, in the case of each individual purchaser, the price of a thing can be taken as a measure of its marginal utility to him. Now to continue.

On the Marshallian view, the law of diminishing utility applies to real income as a whole as well as to individual things. It follows that what Marshall calls the marginal utility of money, i.e. the extra utility which a man can obtain by spending in the most sensible possible way the marginal pound of money income, will be diminished *either* if, prices remaining constant, his money income increases *or* if, his money income remaining constant, its real value is increased by a fall in the price of the particular thing we are studying. On the Marshallian view, the former cause of change must not be neglected, but the latter, generally speaking, can, though in exceptional cases it is necessary to take it into account. Here fits in our old friend the possible effect of the cheapening of an inferior good, say bread, in so increasing a man's real income, and thus so reducing the marginal utility of money to him, as to diminish the amount of the thing bought.

From the fact that utility is measurable in the sense explained, i.e. that the experiencer can say that one *increase* of utility is double another, it does not immediately follow that the *total* utility derived from a thing is measurable in the corresponding sense, i.e. in the sense that the experiencer could say, when he has 200 units of the thing, that his total utility derived therefrom is now $1\frac{1}{2}$ or $1\frac{3}{4}$ or any other definite multiple of what it was when he had 100 units. This sounds a hard saying, but fortunately there is an analogy in the physical world which may help some people. Of the so-called absolute scale of temperature it is possible to say, what it is not possible to say of the ordinary centigrade or Fahrenheit scales, that equal movements along the scale register equal absolute changes of temperature; but it is still not possible to express the total temperature at one point as a multiple of the total temperature at another, so long as the starting-point of the scale is still left unspecified. So it is with utility; and in the case at least of things which are necessary to life, and *a fortiori* in the case of real income as a whole, Marshall is emphatic that we must not take our starting-point for utility at the point where our man's supply of the thing in question is zero but at some higher point. Given, however, that we have fixed on this point in some reasonable way — and for many things it *may* be reasonable to fix it at the point of zero supply – total utility, both in the case of real income as a whole and in the case of each separate constituent of it, becomes *intrinsically* measurable in the same sense as additions to utility are measurable.

The next question is, can we, observing from outside, devise any technique for measuring it? The Marshallian answer is that in the case of real income as a whole we cannot; but that in the case of any individual thing, in principle we can. For if we know the set-up of the man's demand schedule for the thing – let us call it tea – we can estimate what it would be worth his while to pay at each stage rather than have his supply of tea reduced step by step from its present level to the level which we have adjudged to correspond to zero utility. This sum of money, if we are prepared to make one assumption, can be taken as a measure of the total utility to him of tea; and the excess of this sum of money over what he actually *does* pay for his supplies of tea can be taken as the money measure of his 'consumer's surplus' from tea, i.e. of the benefit which he derives from the opportunity of spending part of his income on tea instead of being compelled, by the absence of tea, to spend it all on other things. This measure is none the less a true measure because the possibility of the blackmail process which I have just described being applied is not continuously present in the man's mind, – i.e. because, in common parlance, we seldom realise to the full how much we value a thing, whether it be a fountain pen or a friendship, till we have lost it.

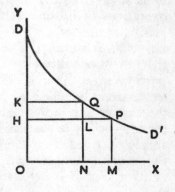

In the picture, a consumer's demand schedule for tea is represented by the curve DD'. Market conditions are such that he is buying OM lb per year at a price of MP(= OH) shillings per lb, thus spending on tea HOMP shillings. The sum which could be extracted from him by the blackmail process just described is DOMP shillings, and – tea being a commodity in respect of which this can sensibly be done – this area is to be regarded as a measure of the total utility, and the triangle DHP as a measure of the consumer's surplus, which he derives from tea.

The assumption of which I spoke just now is that the proportion of the man's whole income which he spends on tea is small; for if it is not, the marginal utility of money to him would be appreciably reduced if part of his income were released from expenditure on tea and became available for expenditure on other things. And in this event money would fail us as a measuring-rod of utility. The passage in which Marshall explains this[1] is not, to me at least, perfectly clear. If you want to torment your supervisors, ask them (i) whether Marshall is suggesting that, in the event supposed, the crude measure of consumer's surplus is too big or too small, (ii) whether he is suggesting that it needs correcting by two separate operations or by one only. I believe you will get a surprising variety of answers! But I do not wish to get hung up unduly over this. The main point for the moment is that on Marshall's view this assumption – that the proportion of income spent on the thing is small – can legitimately be made in most cases, and that therefore, in the case of any individual purchaser, money measures of the total utility of particular things, and of the consumer's surplus derived from them, can sensibly be calculated in the way described and usefully compared with one another. But it is *not* claimed that such measures of the

---

[1] *Principles*, Mathematical Appendix, Note VI.

total utility of particular things can sensibly be added up to yield a measure of the total utility of the man's income. This, however, is not because the total utility of income, in the sense explained in which we take our starting-point somewhere above zero income, is intrinsically or *per se* immeasurable, but simply because our money measuring-rod is not a perfect instrument.

All this being – or so it seems to me – rather difficult, I propose to spend a few minutes in recapitulation, before going farther. I have been drawing two distinctions. (i) The first is the distinction between something being *intrinsically* measurable, in the sense that the experiencer can say which of two wads of it is the greater, and something being *practically* measurable, in the sense that there is some reliable measuring-rod available which the outsider can apply. (ii) The second is the distinction between the *increments* of a thing being measurable, so that one can say that one increment is twice as great as another, and the *whole* of a thing being measurable, so that one can say that one total is twice as great as another total.

I am suggesting that Marshall's view of utility is (1) that increments in it derived from particular things are both intrinsically and practically measurable; (2) that totals of it derived from particular things are not even intrinsically measurable unless you reckon them from a sensible starting-point, but that if you do they *are* intrinsically measurable; (3) that totals derived from particular things are practically measurable with the measuring-rod of money on a certain restrictive assumption, which, however, can generally reasonably be made; but (4) that the total of totals, i.e. the total utility of income in general, is not practically measurable at all.

We have so far been confining our attention to a single purchaser. Our measuring-rod of money is seen to suffer from further imperfections if we try to use it to derive, from the demand schedule of a whole market for a particular thing, a money measure of the consumers' surplus enjoyed from that thing by the whole market. For it is evident that the same sum of money represents different amounts of utility to different people, partly because they differ in tastes and powers of enjoyment, but more importantly because they differ in income; so that we shall be in danger of adding up things which are really incommensurable. In some connections, e.g. if we are trying to compare the community's consumers' surpluses on beer and champagne, or on winkles and oysters, this is obviously very important. But while Marshall's dictum that 'by far the greater number of events with which economics deals affects in about equal proportions all the different members of society' may strike us now as an overstatement, it remains true that there is a large range of cases over which the assumption that the markets for two or more things are made up of different income-classes in about the same proportions can fairly be made.

The upshot then is that even when we cannot make it precise the general notion of consumers' surplus – of the aggregate price paid for a thing not being an adequate measure of what popular language calls its 'true value' and economic jargon its total utility – is of considerable importance as a guide to public policy: and that the more precise we can make it by exact knowledge of the set-up of demand schedules for different things, the more useful it could be. It is, for instance, at the bottom of one of the main arguments – though it is not of course a *decisive* argument – for direct as against indirect taxation; the former leaves it to people to draw in their horns as suits them best, surrendering little flakes of satisfaction in all directions, the latter entails, with no corresponding gain to the State, the surrender of considerable chunks of consumers' surplus on that part of the things selected for

taxation which, as a result of the tax, is no longer bought.[1]
The concept of consumers' surplus is also, as we shall see
later, at the bottom of the argument for the State subsidising or running at a loss certain branches of production,
on the ground that the additional net satisfaction thus
conferred upon consumers will outweigh the loss of
satisfaction represented by the money costs involved.

APPENDIX
[omitted in recent years]

The Marshallian analysis which I have been expounding was of course
developed for a free market, i.e. for a state of affairs in which the consumer
can buy as much of each commodity as he thinks fit. I propose now to add
a short digression about how it has to be modified when a system of
rationing is in force. About a straight rationing system, all that need be
said is that, so far as it is effective, the money measure of the marginal
utility of the rationed commodity stands, for many purchasers, above its
price: but it may be noted in passing that such a situation adds another
difficulty to the use of changes in money national income, corrected by
changes in price-level, as an index of changes in economic welfare. More
tricky is the situation when the consumer has to administer a double
currency of money and points, and finds himself faced, over a certain
range of his expenditure, with a system of point values as well as a system of
money prices. The mathematicians have been having fun with this subject
in recent years (those with strong stomachs may see C. F. Carter in
Economic Journal, December 1948), but I think the gist of what they have
to say can be put fairly intelligibly as follows.

1. If a consumer is administering a double currency of money and
points, the marginal utility of money to him means the addition which
would be made to his total satisfaction by the addition of a 'shilling' to
his money-income, his points-income and the systems of money-prices and
points-prices remaining unchanged. Similarly, the marginal utility of

---

[1] In the picture (p. 75) let us now regard the line HP as signifying that tea can be
produced at an unvarying cost of OH shillings per lb. Let this cost now be raised to OK
by the imposition of a tax HK, thus reducing our consumer's purchases to ON and his
consumer's surplus to DKQ. Then on the ON tea which he still buys he pays a total tax
of KHLQ to the State, which must be presumed to make good use of it. But on the tea
NM which he no longer buys he loses consumer's surplus QLP with no corresponding
gain to the State.

points to him means the addition which would be made to his total satisfaction by the addition of a point to his points-income, his money-income and the systems of money-prices and points-prices remaining unchanged. These two marginal utilities are not, as it were, initially fixed, – they emerge out of the whole pattern of his expenditure (in mathematical language they are among the unknowns which there are enough equations to determine).

2. The consumer will so distribute his expenditure that the utility of the marginal unit of each commodity purchased is equal to the *sum* of its money-price multiplied by the marginal utility of money and its points-price multiplied by the marginal utility of points.

3. The poorer the consumer, the larger is the first term of this sum relatively to the second term, i.e. the larger the part which money-prices play in his decisions. In the extreme case, when the consumer is very poor, and when he cannot hoard his points in the expectation of becoming richer, the marginal utility of points sinks to zero, and the distribution of expenditure is governed entirely by money-prices.

4. Similarly, the richer the consumer the more nearly his expenditure on pointed goods is governed by their relative points-prices. But since there is always *one* non-pointed way of disposing of his income open to him, namely saving it, and probably a number of other non-pointed goods as well, the marginal utility of money cannot sink to zero, so that even the rich man's expenditure on pointed goods is not governed *wholly* by points-prices.

5. For each isolated consumer, the marginal utility of a point thus bears a definite ratio (which, however, in the case of a very poor man may be zero) to the marginal utility of a 'shilling'. This ratio multiplied by a 'shilling' may be called his subjective money-price of points. If now he is brought into contact with a black market and has no inhibitions about dealing in it, he will buy or sell points according as this subjective price of a point exceeds or falls short of the market price, and will carry his transactions up to the limit at which his subjective price becomes equal to the market price. He will then, in distributing his expenditure, act just as he would if he were using money only and if the money-price of each commodity were equal to its actual money-price plus the money equivalent of its points-price.

6. In equilibrium, the market price of points is itself of course determined by the totality of the transactions, and hence ultimately by the make-up of the utility schedules, of all those dealing in it.

It may be added that *discontinuities* are apt to be relatively more prominent in a system of point values than in a system of money-prices, — the points value of a suit of clothes or a pot of golden syrup bears a higher ratio to the points income per period than its money price does even to a moderate money income, so that the maximisation of utility cannot be pursued with great refinement. This increases the practical difficulty of administering a double currency sensibly: nevertheless the problem seems to be solved regularly by millions of not very highbrow people without mental breakdown.

VI

DEMAND AND UTILITY – SOME DIFFICULTIES

I have described what I believe to be the Marshallian assumptions about the sense in which, and the limits within which, utility is measurable in terms of money. And I have expressed my own view that that sense is definite enough, and these limits wide enough, to make the theory of consumers' surplus both intellectually respectable and useful – provided you do not expect too much of it – as a guide to practical action. I must now say something about certain lines of criticism to which this whole set-up has been subjected in recent years. I shall consider three such lines of criticism, in the reverse order, as it seems to me, of their importance.

I

The first takes us back to the rather fiddling matter of the exact nature of the correction which has to be made in the crude money measure of consumers' surplus in those cases in which the proportion of income spent on the thing in question is appreciably great, and a change in the price of the thing accordingly has an effect which cannot be neglected on the marginal utility of income.

This matter has been explored by Professor Hicks in a long series of writings culminating in his 1956 book, *A Revision of Demand Theory*. I have already admitted that I am not entirely clear about Marshall's treatment of the matter; and by the same token I am not entirely clear about the relation of Hicks's treatment to Marshall's. But it seems to me that there are two main differences.

(i) Marshall makes the need for doctoring the crude measure depend on the elasticity of demand for ' tea ': if that happens to be unity over the relevant range, there is no need for doctoring, because no money is either released for, or absorbed from, expenditure on other things. Hicks makes the need for doctoring depend on the price-fall itself, since whether more money is spent on tea as a result, or less, or the same amount, the price-fall increases the man's real income and therefore diminishes its marginal utility.

(ii) Hicks makes plain, in a way that Marshall does not, that the process of doctoring will yield *two* alternative money measures of the increase in the real utility surplus, whose relation may be pictured as follows. Imagine yourself confronted with a fall in the price of tea from QN to PM (figure, p. 75), and laying your plans for increased purchases accordingly. An official comes along and asks you what sum of money you would *accept* as compensation for surrendering the right to take advantage of the fall in the price of tea; and after a little thought you name a sum. Now another fiercer official comes along and tells you your right to buy tea at the new, lower, price has been taken away by the Commissar of Food and that you will be put in prison if you exercise it: and then, melting a little, asks what sum you would be prepared to *pay* to the Commissar of Food as a bribe to rescind this order. And again, after a little thought, you name a sum. Now the first of these two sums will be larger than the second. For if in fact you are not to have the advantage of the fall in price, a shilling will be worth relatively little to you, and you will require a relatively large number of shillings as compensation; while if in fact you are to keep the advantage of the fall in price a shilling will be worth relatively much to you, and you will be prepared to surrender relatively few shillings by way of bribe. These two sums of money — these two alternative measures — will lie one on each side of the crude Marshallian measure, about equidistant from it.

F

The matter perhaps becomes clearer if we allow ourselves for a moment to do what we know we really mustn't do, — namely apply these notions to income as a whole. You are working in a firm in London at a salary of £1,000 a year. The head of the firm asks you what additional salary you would require in order to induce you to work in its branch at Timbuctoo, and you reply £800. Next day he sends for you and orders you to proceed to Timbuctoo at your existing salary; but adds an enquiry what reduction of that salary you would agree to as a price for cancelling the order. Clearly it is very unlikely that you would be ready to name as large a sum as £800.

So far as I can see, these refinements of Hicks (which are somewhat more complicated than I have disclosed to you) are acceptable; but I also think that they are not of great importance, and that the Marshall simplification — 'a simplification of genius', as Hicks himself calls it, — will be adequate for most people's needs.

II

I come to a more serious matter. It is held by some people that utility, like a number of other psychological entities, possesses only what is called 'ordinal' magnitude. According to this view we can take a number of chunks of utility and set them in a row in order of magnitude, labelling them 1, 2, 3 and so on: but the stuff is not of such a kind that we can ever use these numbers as *cardinal* numbers, and say that one chunk contains one unit of utility, another two and another three. In deference to this view the great Italian economist Pareto early in this century worked out an alternative technique for the study of demand, — the technique of 'indifference maps'. Just as you can draw a map putting in contour lines without making any statement about the height of the contours, so you can exhibit the consumer as responding to different price-situations in accordance with his preferences, and can thus give a complete account of what happens in the market, without making any assumption about the *amounts* of utility which the consumer enjoys in the several situations. One can, if one likes, construct an ordered set of numbers corresponding to the total utilities enjoyed in the different situations; but such a 'utility function' is a mere *index* of utility and not a measure of it, and any one out of an indefinitely large number of such series will serve the purpose equally well and be no more or less correct than any other.

Now as I understand it Pareto and his immediate followers did not do their job very thoroughly. They continued to use the law of diminishing marginal utility of individual things and certain other allied propositions with regard to related things, — complements and substitutes. And if you want to do that you have got to assume not only that the consumer is capable of regarding one situation as preferable to another situation, but that he is capable of regarding one *change in situation* as preferable to another *change in situation*. Now while the first assumption doesn't, it appears that the second assumption really *does* compel you to regard utility as being not merely an orderable but a measurable entity.

For if the consumer can compare changes in situation, and can therefore say that he rates the change

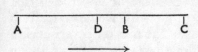

AB more highly than the change BC, it will always be possible to find a point D, such that he rates the change AD *just as highly* as the change DC, and that seems to be equivalent to saying that the interval AC is *twice* the interval AD, — we are back in the world of cardinal measurement.

[I speak for a moment, diffidently, to mathematicians, others closing their ears. Let $\varphi(x)$ be a utility function, in the sense of an index of the total utility enjoyed by a consumer from various amounts of the commodity x. Then if all we want to say is that the consumer prefers a larger amount of x to a smaller amount, so that $\varphi'(x)$ is positive, then any other function $F(\varphi(x))$ will do equally well, provided only that F' is positive, so that $F(\varphi)$ and φ move in the same direction. But if we want to say that the consumer can distinguish between increments of utility, so that, for instance:

$$\varphi(x_3) - \varphi(x_2) < \varphi(x_2) - \varphi(x_1)$$

where x_1, x_2, x_3, are any three successive values of x, then only such functions of x as exhibit this phenomenon are eligible as indices of utility; and it can be shown that any such function $f(x)$ is bound to the original function $\varphi(x)$ by the relation $f(x) = A\,\varphi(x) + B$, where A and B are constants. In other words only two things remain arbitrary about the utility function, — the scale in which we measure (the size of the 'util') and the point from which we start measuring. But this we knew already!]

Thus some years ago there set in a great hue and cry among the Paretians to remove the offending odour of utility which Pareto had left hanging about the house. At one time this movement of thought seemed to be leading its adherents into the sterile position that economics had got nothing to do with welfare at all; if you can explain what happens in the market by observing people's reactions to total situations, why bother to go further? From this dead end they, or some of them, seem now to have been rescued largely by the activities of Professor Hicks, who has contrived, to his own and a number of other people's satisfaction, to re-establish 'welfare economics', and more particularly to re-enthrone (though in the more complicated form which I have just mentioned) the money measurement of consumers' surplus as a guide to policy in various fields, without avowedly using the concept of measurable utility at all.

In his earlier book *Value and Capital* Hicks's treatment involved making an assumption about the convexity of those 'indifference curves' which appeared to some of us to involve the reintroduction of marginal utility in disguise. In his 1956 book, he appears to have accepted, with modifications, a reformulation of the whole matter by Samuelson which is stated, as so modified, to demand no further assumption than that (1) the consumer always acts, in different situations, in accordance with a *consistent* scale of preferences, (2) given his supplies of all other things, he would always rather have more money than less. Samuelson and his followers, by the way, are, or were some time ago, still somewhat sceptical of Hicks's claims to have rehabilitated welfare economics, and in his big book Samuelson used language about one of Hicks's achievements which seemed to come very near denouncing him as a Benthamite cardinalistic deviationist!

There has been a flood of literature on all this in the last few years. I have said my say on such of it as I can understand, and have given many references, in my two articles, 'Utility and All That' (in the book so named) and 'Utility and All What' (in the book *Economic Commentaries*). Broadly, I still take leave to think that Marshall, in conceding that we cannot even in principle measure the total utility of our whole supplies of primary necessities, and also that we cannot in practice measure in money the sum of the total utilities of a large number of different things, has taken in advance most of the sting out of the attack on the concept of measurable utility. I do not deny that a reasonable account of the behaviour of the individual consumer can be built up without its aid; though I think that even in this field an analysis which makes use of it gives a more persuasive account of what really happens than one which does not. I think too that once we have armed ourselves with a law of diminishing utility of income in the case of the individual, we can go on to make with some confidence, for most of the purposes with which economists are concerned, those comparisons between the economic welfare of different persons which the modern purists forbid us to make, or rather tell us that, if we insist on making them, we are ceasing to act as economists and basing ourselves on ethical considerations. I do not think that is right, – I think such judgments are judgments of fact, though doubtless rough ones. In making them, we must indeed recognise that individuals differ in their powers of enjoyment; but for many broad purposes of economic policy we can fairly assume that these differences in susceptibility are distributed in a random fashion between income-groups, so that the only differences in the satisfaction-bearing power of a pound which we need, or can, attempt to take into account are those arising out of differences in family income. This of course points to something not far from complete equality of distribution as the ideal method of generating the maximum of positive utility out of a given real national income, at any rate if *time* is given to soften the effect of transfers of income. But of course it does not follow that we should aim at complete equality if we think that the attempt to attain it, by impairing the incentives to work and save, would seriously reduce the size of the income to be distributed; nor again if we think that the economic arguments for equality, i.e. those based on the idea of the maximisation of economic welfare, are outweighed by ethical, or even by what we may call in the broadest sense aesthetic, arguments on the other side.

But you will have to explore for yourselves at leisure so much of the highbrow literature in this field as you can stomach. And you will doubtless find it useful to acquire, from one of the many textbooks which expound it, that technique of 'indifference curves' of which I shall not myself attempt in these lectures to make use.

III

The third line of criticism to be met goes, I think, deeper, and takes us back to the assumption of rational behaviour on the part of the consumer. How far is it justified? You will recall that it consists of two sub-assumptions, — first that we desire things in proportion to the satisfaction which we expect to get from them, and secondly that the satisfaction which we *do* get is equal to the satisfaction we expected to get. Neither of these things is always true. There are notoriously some things of which it may be said that they are

> Enjoy'd no sooner but despised straight,
> Past reason hunted and, no sooner had,
> Past reason hated, as a swallowed bait
> On purpose laid to make the taker mad.

But short of such extreme cases it is frequently argued that in modern times the arts of the salesman and the advertiser have reached such a pitch that many people are chronically in the position of buying things which they don't really want and as to the satisfaction-giving power of which they are being skilfully misled. 'The National Association of Kraut Manufacturers', so I once read somewhere, 'has made America sauerkraut-conscious in the short space of two years, thus redeeming the odium on one of God's gifts to mankind': but is America really the happier in consequence? We shall have to return to these considerations later when we come to discuss the organisation of production and trade. How big a hole they make in the theory of consumers' choice and consumers' surplus each person must judge for himself; but it is generally agreed that in certain fields, such as medicine, the hole is big enough to need a certain amount of plugging by protective legislation, modifying the general rule of *caveat emptor*.

More important perhaps is the fact that many human satisfactions depend on convention and fashion. Thus my demand for, and satisfaction derived from, evening clothes depends principally on how many other people have got them, and *what* other people have got them, my maximum state of pleasure being reached when the other possessors are neither too many nor too few, and are the right people and not the wrong. The surrender of my evening clothes, other people retaining theirs, would involve me in a big loss of consumer's surplus; but if all of us made a plot never to wear such things, as we did during the war, it may be that we should none of us be significantly worse off. Perhaps many consumers' surpluses are rather like bubbles, – they are real things, but easily pricked; or like the claws of a lobster, – *uno avulso non deficit alter* – new ones grow fairly easily if old ones are lopped off. But it is important that they *should* grow again; for a lobster without claws is a poor animal, and a world without consumers' surpluses would be, for most of us, a dull place.

If some market demands do not come to very much in the way of realised utilities, the converse is also true. It is generally agreed that there are some important utilities for the realisation of which it is not safe or practicable to trust to the operation of market demand. Among such are, at the very least, the prime necessities of protection from enemies abroad, from violence, robbery and injustice at home, from pestilence due to lack of sanitation. And to these, nations of the type with which we are chiefly concerned decided a good many years ago to add protection from damage owing to one's neighbour's children failing to receive adequate care and instruction, – a decision the full implications of which we have perhaps not yet realised. Again there are a number of cases, notably the provision of roads, where the play of individual demand can perhaps be relied on to evoke service of a kind, but the method of individual payment according to service rendered is found intolerably inconvenient. In all these cases, if utilities are to be effectively realised, it must be through the route of communal consumption, organised by collective action and paid for otherwise than through the market. On one ground and another, the drift of modern practice has been towards a large increase in the range of physical and cultural services thrust down the throat, or at any rate dangled before the nose, of the citizen consumer on this plan. Evidently there is room for large differences of judgment on how far these principles can usefully be carried; for clearly of the loss or gain of utility achieved by superseding the market there can be no market test. Some for instance might say that with our modern knowledge of dietetics the expert, if he were given his head, could create bigger realised surpluses of satisfaction from food for the consumer than the latter will ever succeed in creating for himself. Others will harp impenitently on its being the little bit of what you fancy that does you good, and insist that the proper function of the expert is to *inspire* intelligent choices and not to make them.

As we all know only too well, in war or war-induced scarcity it is imperative, both for physical and psychological reasons, to take the distribution between families of many particular goods outside, or partially outside, the jurisdiction of the purse and the market. But there may well be a tendency for such arrangements to outlive their usefulness just because they furnish an unobtrusive channel for the redistribution of real income. It seems to me desirable that in normal times a community, whether it be individualist or socialist or something betwixt and between, should keep as distinct as possible in its head the two separate questions 'On what principles do we desire that real income shall be distributed between families?' and 'How far is it expedient and economical to consume communally and how far through the device of individual purchase at honest prices?' My own disposition has long been to believe that we should welcome the extension of the principle of communalised demand in certain selected directions but look very critically at it in others, particularly in the large and important realms of housing and food, and should indeed aim at being in a position to reverse the gears and to revert to a position where the citizen spender is treated as an adult and responsible person, free, with certain intelligible exceptions, from thumping purchase taxes on the one hand and undignified subsidies on the other. I therefore welcome the steps which have been taken in this direction in this country in recent years. In any case, to revert to the immediate theme of this lecture, let us hang on to the doctrine of measurable consumers' surplus as embodying a true word about the end and aim of economic activity, and as a bulwark not by any means against all interferences with 'things as they are' – on the contrary there are some for which it provides a rational and powerful sanction – but against *fussy* and *messy* interferences which ride roughshod over the valuable variety of human tastes and aspirations.

VII

DEMAND, SUPPLY AND COMPETITIVE VALUE

We return to the main thread of the story, which I shall assume you to be following in the pages of Marshall IV and V, – taking advantage, perhaps, of his own suggestion to omit V, 8 to 11, at a first reading, but supplementing the remainder with the Chapter II, 1, of his later book *Industry and Trade* in which he tried to summarise, for the benefit of the non-academic reader, the teaching of the *Principles*.

What determines the relative value of different things? The theory of demand tells us that the demand of a market for a thing is not a fixed quantity but a quantity in relation to a price, so that it can only be expressed accurately as a series of conditional sentences:

(1) If a is the price per unit, x is the quantity demanded;
  „ b „ „ y „ „
  „ c „ „ z „ „

Or, putting the same thing in another way,

(2) If x is the quantity available, a is the selling price per unit;
  „ y „ „ b „ „
  „ z „ „ c „ „

If then we know the quantity available, we know which of the above statements under (2) is relevant to the actual condition of affairs. We can fill out ' Value depends on demand and supply' into 'Value depends primarily on the conditions of demand and on quantity available, and measures the utility to the purchaser of that part of the quantity available which just finds a purchaser'.

This is the end of the story as regards things whose supply is fixed by natural or historical causes, usually illustrated by pictures by Raphael[1] (though of course the supply even of these may be increased by the vagaries of art-critics or diminished, e.g., by war). That might be true too of ordinary things in an effectively cut-off market, such as a besieged city. More important, it may be true also of ordinary things in *any* market *for the moment*, usually illustrated by fish in a fish-market on Saturday night. Hence our statement is the last word about *competitive market value*. At least, nearly the last word: for, even at the moment, demand is influenced by estimates of the quantity likely to become available in the near future, in the light of which the buyer has *some* power of choice whether to buy or to hold back. And unless the thing is very perishable, the seller too can choose whether to hold back stocks or to press them on the market, – the quantity 'available' is not the same thing as the quantity in existence. Thus future supplies exert their influence on present value.

Further we must of course as economists go behind the immediate market situation and ask why this quantity and not some other has become available. The method I propose to follow is to fly to the opposite extreme, and to lay down and analyse the long-run law of competitive value, which may be stated as follows.

The value of a thing produced under conditions of free competition tends in the long run to equal its average cost of production per unit.

The development of this proposition will occupy us a long time, so some preliminary remarks on it require careful notice.

(1) 'Tends in the long run to equal', not 'equals'. We must not think of the 'long-run value' of a thing as something which will be attained after so many months or years and then stay put. It is more nearly legitimate to

---

[1] Or by such other artist as the text-book writer thinks will most impress the reader with the modernity of his taste.

think of it as a norm around which actual value oscillates, as a pendulum does about a vertical line, or a 'sine curve' about a horizontal one, so that even though the moments when value actually equals cost of production are few, yet whenever it diverges from it a force, which will ultimately be victorious, is at work tending to bring it back again. Yet even that conception, though helpful, may be too clear-cut for application to a changing world. It may be that in such a world long-run equilibrium is *never* attained. It is the state of affairs which *would* be attained if all the forces at work had time to work themselves out; but it may be that in any particular case they never *will* have time to work themselves out, since other events, altering the whole set-up, will have occurred before they do.[1]

This concept of long-period equilibrium appears to be found puzzling by some people. Mrs Robinson, indeed, in a fairly recent article (*Review of Economic Studies*, No. 55, p. 84) speaks of it as a 'profound methodological error which makes the larger part of neo-classical doctrine spurious'. 'It is impossible', she continues, 'for a system to *get into* a position of equilibrium, for the very nature of equilibrium is that the system is already in it, and has been in it for a certain length of past time.'

With respect, after taking the best philosophical advice open to me, this sentence seems to me great nonsense. It is true that if we say that a body was 'at rest' in position P at time X, that implies that it was in the position P for some period of time, even if only a very short one, either just before X or just after X; but that does not mean that it is not possible for a body in motion to become at rest, — plainly it *is* possible. And what I have just said of the concepts 'body' and 'at rest' appears to me to be equally true of the concepts 'system' and 'in equilibrium'. There seems to be no more reason for saying that the idea of a

[1] See Guillebaud, listed article, pp. 111 ff.

system being in equilibrium implies that the system actually *is* in equilibrium than for saying that the idea of heaven implies that we are already in it, or even that we ever shall be. For while it seems to me plainly possible for a system to get into equilibrium, it also seems to me very important that, as I have already emphasised, it *may* never succeed in doing so. It seems to me that anybody who rejects these two ideas, that a system can move towards equilibrium and that it may never actually get into it, has not only failed to understand Marshall's teaching but has made it extremely difficult for himself to interpret the course of events in the real world.

We can make some approach to definiteness by distinguishing broadly between periods of time in which the rate of supply of the thing we are considering can be altered, but the equipment and organisation required for making it cannot ('short' periods); and periods in which the equipment and organisation can also be altered in amount, upwards or downwards ('long' periods). We start, as already said, by attempting to take these latter changes into account, i.e. by studying long-period value. And for brevity I shall often say that value *is* or *does* such and such, when what I mean is that it *tends to be or do* such and such when these slowly moving forces are taken into account.

(2) 'Under free competition', which notoriously doesn't always prevail, though even nowadays often perhaps comes nearer to prevailing in the long run than might appear at first sight. But what exactly do we mean by it? Marshall, I think, meant primarily that the *processes* of competition were actively at work. But under the influence of mathematical habits of thought, it has become customary to say that a *purely* competitive situation only exists if each seller takes the price ruling in the market as something given, which he cannot affect by altering his own output; his only business is to decide how much

to sell at that price. If he raised his price ever so little above the prevailing price, he would lose all his custom, if he lowered it ever so little he would find himself able to sell more than ever he could bring to market. Thus whatever the shape of the whole demand curve for the thing in question, the demand curve facing the individual supplier must be pictured as a horizontal straight line. At the opposite extreme stands complete monopoly, where a single supplier controls the whole output of the thing, so that the demand curve for the whole output and that for *his* output are identical.

Evidently this conception of competition is a very rigid one. In particular, if logically adhered to, it rules out a number of activities which are commonly thought of as highly competitive; for it entails the consequence that the producer, in order to sell all he desires, need incur no costs of transport, marketing or advertisement beyond, presumably, a certain minimum necessary to place his wares in some central spot and to make their presence there known to potential buyers (e.g. even under 'pure' competition the cost of running a motor-van to, and hiring a stall in, the Cambridge market would fail to be met by the village producer of vegetables). This is of course a very inadequate picture of real life; and some people prefer to start by building up a general theory of value in an imperfect market, taking pure competition as an extreme special case. In my view this method turns out to be fuller of bogs and pitfalls than was appreciated when it first became fashionable some years ago; and if one is going to try to improve on Marshall by being more formal and precise than he cared to be, the methodological advantage is still, I think, on the side of starting with pure competition as a standard of reference; then taking monopoly as a secondary standard of reference; and then saying what can be said about the spectrum of cases lying in between.

It is worth noting also that, if we are interested in what ought to be as well as what is, the notion of a 'fair' price[1] is historically closely bound up with the notion of cost under fully competitive conditions; though it is not true, as we shall see, that such conditions always necessarily produce the best results from the point of view of society.

(3) 'Cost' means simply 'money cost'. We are assuming stability, in some sense, in the general value of money, so we need not at present distinguish between costs in terms of money and in terms of commodities. And we postpone till much later the question of how far these money costs measure 'real' costs or disutilities such as we studied in Crusoe-land. But there will come a point when, in order to draw useful inferences, we shall have to distinguish between increases in costs which are due to the drawing of additional resources into a given branch of production and those which represent additional payments to resources already there.

With these preliminary remarks let us return to our proposition, – the value of a thing under competition tends in the long run to equal its average cost of production per unit. To develop it, we need a new concept, – that of supply price. The supply price of a given annual output of a thing can be defined for the present as the price which just suffices to evoke that annual output: though we shall find that we have to make this definition a little more complicated later on. Using this *definition*, we make an *assertion*, namely that the supply price of a given output tends to equal the average cost of production per unit when that output is being produced. The reason is that if a higher price than this average cost prevails some or all of the sellers will be making an unlooked-for gain; there will be an inducement to other persons to

[1] Some such word as fair, due, reasonable or their opposites was used thirty-two times, without explanation, in seven pages in the Report of an anti-profiteering committee of 1920.

enter the industry, thus adding to the output; and in order to absorb the increased output the price will have to go down again. On the other hand if a lower price than the average cost prevails, some sellers will be unable to cover their total costs, and will sooner or later move to other industries or be driven out of business. Hence output will be reduced and demand price rise, i.e. the competition of buyers for the reduced supply will drive the price up again.

This supply price will usually be different for different outputs, i.e. we have, as in the case of demand, a set of conditional sentences:

(1) *If* a is the price offered, x is the output evoked;
„ b   „   „   y   „   „
„ c   „   „   z   „   „

And, using our proposition that supply price equals average cost per unit, we can, as in the case of demand, turn the thing round and say

(2) *If* x is the output, a is the average cost per unit;
„ y „   „   b   „   „
„ z „   „   c   „   „

Both these ways of looking at the thing will be found useful: though, once more, the first set of sentences is not so innocent as it looks, and will have to be more precisely phrased later.

We can now sum up provisionally by combining our theories of demand and supply. The price at which a thing is sold, and the quantity produced and sold, depend in the long run *both* on the conditions of demand *and* on the conditions of supply. The price must equal *both* the marginal demand price *and* the average cost of production; the quantity must be such as *both* can be absorbed by the market at the prevailing price, *and* remuneratively brought to market at the price. A pound of tea, say, bears a price twice that of a pound of cheese, *both* because a small addition to the supply of tea would add twice as

G

much to the satisfaction of consumers (so far as that can be measured in money) as a small addition to the supply of cheese, *and* because the expense of production (so far as *that* can be measured in money) is twice as great. Both statements are true, neither alone is complete.

We may illustrate from the difficulties which beset attempts to fix maximum prices, as during the war. If you (you being the Government) fix a price, say CE = FG, lower than the normal price AB, you encounter two difficulties. The first shows itself forthwith. You have en-

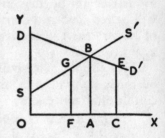

couraged the satisfaction of demands which, as expressed in money, are less insistent than those which it was just possible to satisfy before: the quantity demanded at price CE exceeds the quantity available, and a scramble ensues. If money demand is not a perfect index of social need, neither is degree of intimacy with the grocer or power to stand without fainting in a queue. And price-fixing breaks down unless you go on to *ration*. The second difficulty shows itself more slowly: but by fixing a price (FG) lower than cost of production for the existing scale of output, you are encouraging producers to sell illicitly, to hoard stocks, to turn to producing something which is uncontrolled, or to go out of business. Thus the rate of available output sinks even further below the rate of demand at the fixed price, and the scramble is intensified. And price-fixing breaks down unless you go on at the least to extend it over a very wide range of commodities, and probably ultimately to assume responsibility for the supply either by subsidising private persons or by producing the thing yourself.

VIII

THE FACTORS OF PRODUCTION AND THEIR COMBINATION

Once more, then, we have arrived at a solution of the problem of value which is satisfactory so far as it goes: but it does not yet go very far. Why does one thing cost twice as much, or ten times as much, to produce per lb weight as another? What *are* these costs of production?

The cost of producing – in the broad sense – a given quantity of a thing can be analysed in at least two ways. The first is according to the nature of the result wrought by the productive power expended. On this method we can distinguish between four main operational stages of 'production' in the broad sense, viz. (1) extraction from Nature, by the processes of agriculture, mining, etc; (2) alteration in shape and texture, by the processes of manufacture; (3) carriage through space – the operation of transport; (4) carriage through time by the operations of trading and dealing, – which often also contain an element of (3), while both (3) and (4) may be partially interposed between (1) and (2) and between the various sub-stages thereof, as well as supervening at the end of the story. If we were conducting a realistic enquiry into the price of a particular article, it would be natural to proceed by trying to disentangle these stages and see how much of the final cost was to be attributed to each of them.

But for our purpose of a broad survey of the forces determining value, the other method of analysis is more illuminating. This is to analyse the total cost of production of the thing into the cost of remunerating the various *factors* or *agents* of *production* which contribute to its making and placing on the market. Now just as there is no clear line between one 'thing' or product and another, so there is no clear line between one factor and another. As with products so with factors, if we want to emphasise those differences between classes of objects which prevent them from being perfectly interchangeable with one another, we shall have to make our classification elaborate and detailed; if we are content for the purpose in hand to blur and soft pedal all but very major differences, we can make the classification broad and simple. In my view, if we are ever to get anywhere, we must start by adopting this latter course, even if we find that we are driven to refine on it later.

The traditional broad classification of factors was a threefold one, – into Land, Capital and Labour: to which Marshall rightly added a fourth, Organisation, perhaps better described as Enterprise. Perhaps a tidier method of approach would be to say that there are two prime agents, Nature and Man, and that Man's activities are of three kinds – working, by hand or brain, 'waiting' or 'going without', the activity lying behind Capital, and taking the *risks* of loss or failure. But the fourfold classification has its conveniences, especially in its rough correspondence to the familiar categories of income, – rent, interest, wages and profits. We shall be very much concerned with these agents or factors later on in connection with the theory of the distribution of income, and anything said about them now must be taken as provisional. But for purposes of discussion of the theory of value, we need to have a working picture of them in our mind's eye.

'By *Land*', says Marshall, 'is meant the materials and the forces which Nature gives freely for man's aid, in land and water, in air and light and heat', – to which of course we must now add intra-atomic energy. As so defined, the most obvious characteristic of Land is that it cannot be increased by human action, even though, as in Holland, the number of acres of solid earth is being increased; it seems to be doubtful whether it is equally true, as used to be stated, that it cannot be diminished. Man seems to be pretty good, as the Dust Bowl in North America for instance bears witness, at *destroying* the free gifts of Nature, though by definition he cannot create them.

Evidently too Land as so defined is often – e.g. in the Cambridgeshire fen land reclaimed in the seventeenth century – so mixed up with other factors that there is no great point in trying to disentangle it, even in thought. But the connections in which the peculiar features of Land *are* relevant do not seem to be diminishing in importance. For, on the demand side, even more fundamental than the quality of fertility are those attributes somewhat pompously described as 'extension and support'. Extension, – the quality emphasised by that not negligible economist Adolf Hitler in his catchword of 'lebensraum', reminding us that *room* is necessary for the display of every human activity, from moneychanging at one end of the scale to deer-stalking or bombing-practice at the other. Support, – an attribute, like consumers' surplus, seldom clearly realised till it is withdrawn, as when buildings subside owing to underground mining, or a ship goes down at sea, or an aircraft encounters bumps and pockets in the air. And on the supply side we have the feature not only of fixity of total supply but of *immobility*, – you can't shift land about if there is too much of it in one place and not enough of it in another.[1] Hence there seem to be good reasons for continuing to class Land as a separate factor.

As regards *Capital*, however we decide in the end to use the word, it is well to start by distinguishing clearly certain concepts in the mind.

(i) There is first the activity of deliberately going

---

[1] Here again, the phenomenon of divertible rain-clouds may serve to remind us how difficult it is ever to tell the strict truth.

without immediate consumption to which a man has a legal right, which in the kind of society which we are considering may be regarded as being normally, though not always, the counterpart in some sense to the growth of the society's material wealth.

(i) There is secondly the concept of bundles of rights to consume, existing in the form of money, and usable by the owner to build up material wealth, or transferable by him to other people – including Governments – who desire either to consume beyond their income, or to build up material wealth. This is sometimes called free or floating capital, or command over capital, or loanable or investible funds.

(iii) There is thirdly the concept of society's stock of man-made material wealth, or rather of that part of it which is directed to the purpose of further production. This limitation gives rise to difficulties of definition precisely analogous to those which we had to face in connection with the national income, – difficulties which have to be solved in the same sort of common-sense way, e.g. by deciding that a house is always capital, but that a chair or a motor-car being used by the owner is wealth but not capital. As so conceived, the kinds of capital can be reduced to two, – fixed capital and circulating or (I think better) working capital. About the former there is no difficulty, – it obviously includes *instruments* of all kinds, including buildings, and improvements to land such as drainage works or harbours. About the latter, the point to realise is that it does not consist mainly, as it might in a Crusoe or other very simple economy, of stores of consumable goods set aside to live on while fixed capital is being constructed, though it *includes* such stores. But under a régime of division of labour such stores need not be very considerable, since A can make steam-engines while B and C make bread and shirts *concurrently*. What working capital is, then, is the whole mass of goods *in process*, i.e. somewhere on their way from the soil to the consumer or ultimate user, – including some goods, such as coal or manure, which do not reach the consumer in recognisable form at all but are destroyed in the productive process.

(iv) Finally we have to be on the look-out for a fourth concept, – the concept of capital which is arrived at by taking the standpoint of the individual instead of, as we have done in (iii), the whole society. The sum of an individual's private assets includes material objects, within which we must draw, as before, an arbitrary line between those which it is convenient to regard as capital and those which it is not. It includes also, or may include, some of those claims which we have classified as floating capital or investible funds. But it is apt nowadays to consist predominantly of claims of other kinds, some of them, such as shares or debentures, having a counterpart in existing material objects, but others, such as most holdings of Government debt, having none.

It is, I think myself, a mistake to try to tie down too rigidly to a single use a word which has so many shades of meaning in ordinary life. But the consequences of not doing so may be unfortunate. Thus Keynes's critique of Marshall's theory of interest (*General Theory*, appendix to Chapter 14) seems to me to miss the mark altogether, because he elects to suppose that Marshall must be using the word capital in the third of my three senses, – the sense of concrete capital objects, whereas to me it seems obvious that Marshall is using it in the second sense, – 'command over capital' or investible funds. Undeterred by Marshall's, as I think, unmerited fate, I propose to use the word, so far as it is required for expounding the theory of value, in a sense which wobbles common-sensibly between (ii) a homogeneous flow of funds and (iii) a heterogeneous collection of instruments. But I promise to return to these difficulties later in the year.

About *Labour* – work by hand or brain – there is nothing particular more to say at this stage, for everybody has a pretty clear idea of what is meant by it.

Enterprise is a composite factor, combining work of a particular kind, provision of capital, and exposure of that capital to risk of loss and chance of gain. The particular compound most easy to identify and argue about is that found in the owner of, or partner in, a private business, who was the typical figure in British industry a hundred years ago, and has got firmly into the books, including Marshall's *Principles*. It is more difficult to put one's finger on this factor in the joint-stock form of organisation dominant today in many fields, though even now not in all. So far as the essential element is the bearing of risk, it is still with the proprietors, that is the shareholders, including the directors so far as they are considerable shareholders. So far as the essential element is the exercise of unfettered decision, it is rather with the directors, and probably not with all of them, – perhaps with the Chairman alone or in association with one or more managing directors, or sometimes (especially in America, where he is often dignified with the name of President) with the salaried general manager. In some cases, and not only those in which all or most of the ordinary shares are in family hands, the legal form of the joint-stock company covers a personal autocracy not much less complete than in the old days. In others the shareholders, perhaps after having lain dormant for a long time, may intermittently reassert their rights of ultimate control. Nowadays we have to take account too, even in the 'Western' economies which we are studying, of the nationally owned industries or part-industries. Here the risk-bearing function lies with the taxpayer, while the supreme decision-making power may be parcelled out between a Public Board, a Minister and his civil servants, and the Legislature, in a manner which is often far from clearly laid down.

It must be conceded that the theory of business enterprise and its reward profits needs continual re-scrutiny in the light of the changing forms of business organisation. Nevertheless for many purposes of broad analysis, no great mischief is likely to result from continuing to speak, as I shall often do, of 'the entrepreneur' or 'the business man'.

Our question: What constitutes the total cost of producing say x pairs of boots per year resolves itself into the two following questions: (1) What determines the cost per unit of each of these four factors of production? (2) What determines the amount of the services of each of them which is used in producing x pairs of boots per year? If we can answer these questions, we shall know why the total cost of producing x pairs of boots per year, and therefore the average cost per unit when x pairs are produced, is what it is and neither more nor less.

For the first three factors we can solve both these questions provisionally by adopting the standpoint of an individual entrepreneur.

(1) As an individual master-bootmaker I shall have to pay for each factor the price my fellow bootmakers are paying, otherwise I shan't obtain the use of it. For me the price is determined by what they are paying. But we can tentatively go further and say, as an approach shot to the full truth (we have learnt by now, I hope, not to be contemptuous about such), that the price which all of us bootmakers have to pay for these factors is governed by what is being paid, quality for quality, *in other industries*. We shall none of us be able to hire land in the middle of a town for £50 an acre if shopkeepers and cinema-builders are offering £60 an acre for similar sites. We shall none of us be able to borrow money at 4 per cent if the Government is issuing loans at 5 per cent; nor, for long, to hire skilled workmen at £8 a week if the clothing and engineer-

ing trades are paying £10. Thus as a first approximation, which we shall have to qualify later, the cost of land, labour and capital to any individual trade, as well as to any individual employer, is governed by the conditions prevailing in the industry of the country as a whole. And it is pretty clear, from what we know of ordinary commodities, that the fact that these things bear a price indicates that they are *scarce* relatively to the desire to make use of them.

(2) What determines the quantity of each of these factors which I, as a bootmaker, shall employ in my business? The answer may be indicated in rough common-sense language by saying that I shall employ each of them with one eye on its efficiency and the other on its cost; but to get more precision, we must examine two of the most formidable-looking Principles of Economics, – the Law of Diminishing Return and the Principle of Substitution.

The corpses of dead controversies with which the path of the economist is strewn lie specially thick in the domain of the twin ogres, the Laws of Diminishing and Increasing Return. We are concerned at the moment mainly with the former, and in only one, but that the most fundamental, of its several possible meanings. It tells us that if successive increments of one factor are employed in conjunction with a fixed stock of all the others, these increments will, after a point, yield successively smaller and smaller additions to the total product. This crabbed and abstract statement is of course well based on common sense and experience. If a farmer takes on extra acres, working with his existing labour force, stock of ploughs, etc., he will have to cultivate each acre less intensively and therefore with less good results. If he takes on more labour without enlarging his farm or capital equipment, each successive man will be employed on less and less urgent tasks and under more and more unfavourable conditions, and so make a smaller and smaller addition to the product.

Up to a point, indeed, the opposite state of affairs may hold good, if there is some indivisible unit of one or more of the existing factors which is not being used up to capacity, — say the entrepreneur himself or some large and expensive machine. Our farm *may* be manifestly too small in area, or understaffed, or understocked. But *after a point* the law of diminishing return, in our present sense, is universal and inevitable, and applies to all factors of production and in all industries.

Observe that, except in extreme cases, there will be *some* addition to the total product, — the added increment of the factor will not, permanently, stand idle because there is no possible way of using it. It is said, I am never sure with what truth, that labour in an Indian village *does* constitute such an exception, its marginal product being virtually nil or even negative. But normally, the technical methods of production not being rigidly fixed, some *substitution* is possible of one factor for others, e.g. when extra labour is employed on a farm as just described, each bushel of wheat will be the result of rather more labour and less land than before, — labour will have been substituted for land to some extent in its make-up. What the law states is that this substitutability is not complete: an extra dose of labour alone is not 'as good as' an extra dose of labour, land, etc., combined. Indeed, if it were, the logical purist can say that it would not be sensible to class labour and land, any more than fair-haired men and dark-haired men, as separate factors of production: though I think myself we could perhaps still find common-sense reasons for doing so.

The individual organiser, then, can form a pretty shrewd idea of the addition which he can make to his output — and so, taking the price for granted, to its selling-value — by taking on a little more of one factor of production. This expected addition to the value of the product constitutes the limit to what he will pay for a small extra supply of the factor,– it is in fact his demand price for it. And we can draw up a statement of his demand on the usual lines.

If x is the amount of the factor he uses, a is its marginal productivity to him, and his demand price for it;

If y is the amount of the factor he uses, b is its marginal productivity to him, and his demand price for it;

If z is the amount of the factor he uses, c is its marginal productivity to him, and his demand price for it;

And as with consumers' demand, we can turn the thing round, and say

If a is the price of the factor, x is the amount of it which he will use;

„ b   „   „   y   „   „   „

„ c   „   „   z   „   „   „

Thus the cost of the factor is, as we know, determined for him by what it can command in other firms and trades: it is for him to push its use up that point at which its marginal productivity coincides with the price he has to pay; beyond this point it will not pay him to employ it. He will do this for each several factor; in other words he will employ that combination of them which enables him to produce a given output at least aggregate cost, or (in other words again) to produce the largest output for a given aggregate cost.

This is what Marshall (V, 4) calls 'applying the principle of substitution' – which is simply the producer's variant of that principle of equi-marginal return which we found at work in Crusoe's case and in that of the ordinary consumer. But the phrase is perhaps a little misleading, for it suggests that, if the price of one factor falls, the entrepreneur will necessarily find it advantageous to employ a smaller absolute amount of one or more of the other factors. This *may* be so: for instance, as we shall see later, a fall in the price of capital may induce particular entrepreneurs to employ less labour, substituting machinery. But it is by no means necessary that substitution should take place in this absolute sense. A cheapening of one factor, say capital, *may* so cheapen the product and extend its sales as to raise the entrepreneur's demand schedule for *all* other factors, and hence the amount of them he employs. In this case he will not, in one sense, be substituting capital for any other factor; but in another sense he will. For the amount which he employs of other factors, which have not been cheapened, will not increase *as much as* the amount which he employs of capital, which has: so that inside each unit of output, as it were, there has been substitution of capital for the other factors, just as in the case posited in our formulation of the law of diminishing return when the amount of the other factors was supposed to remain fixed.

By such processes is the quantity of each factor hired by the individual entrepreneur, and hence the quantity employed in the whole industry, determined. Evidently there are great differences between industries in respect of the relative productivity of the various factors: e.g. in coal-mining or high-grade tailoring the productivity of labour is high as compared with that of capital and the bulk of the cost of the product is labour-cost: in oil-refining or electricity supply the reverse.

Now can we extend this analysis to the fourth factor, business enterprise? There are obvious difficulties so long as we continue to look at a single firm. For then we cannot apply the law of diminishing return to such a lumpy unit as a whole business man; we cannot estimate his marginal productivity by subtracting what the business would produce without a head from what it actually does produce, for the former might well be zero. Nor can we easily picture him applying the principle of substitution to himself in the light of his own cost to himself.

Nevertheless it would seem that, if we take up the standpoint of the whole industry, the law of diminishing return and the principle of substitution can after all be seen at work. Given the amount of other factors in an industry, there is a limit (varying greatly between different industries) in the number of independent business men under whom they can profitably be organised. In other words there comes a point after which each addition to the supply of business men would make a smaller and smaller addition to the total product of the industry; thus there is, as it were, a descending demand curve from the industry for business enterprise just as there is for capital or labour.

Similarly, the cost of an industry of a business man of given efficiency is what he could earn elsewhere, just as in the case of labour or capital. If his marginal productivity falls below his cost, the forces of competition and industrial change will tend to push him out into other industries or into the ranks of hired management, that is of skilled labour of a particular kind. Thus these forces are applying the principle of substitution to him in the same sort of way that he is applying it to the other factors. Hence neither as regards cost per unit nor as regards quantity employed in an industry does enterprise differ from the other factors so much as might at first appear.

Thus we have reached another halting-place. We have found that under competition the value of a thing in the long run tends to equal its average cost of production per unit, which depends on the costliness of the various factors and the quantity of each employed. The former depends on the demand for the factors over the whole field of industry and on the quantity of them available; the latter depends, given their cost per unit, on their technical efficiency relatively to one another in the industry in question. And we can round off the matter, and at the same time leave a loose thread to be taken up later, by saying that the value of each factor tends to equal its marginal productivity, this being equal in all uses.

But having painted this agreeably simple picture, we must now, alas, proceed to blur its outlines by returning to a consideration of the behaviour of our supply schedule.

IX

INCREASING AND DECREASING COST

Our supply curve is a set of conditional sentences, show-ing – in one aspect – for various rates of output the average cost of production which would exist if that rate of output were established. Over a certain range, at any rate, for any industry the curve may either rise or fall. What are the reasons for this?

(1) INCREASING COST

At first sight it is hard to see how it can rise. For we are allowing plenty of time for things to work themselves out, and we have supposed our industry to be able to take on unlimited quantities of the factors of production (including business ability) at prices determined outside itself: and if this is so, there seems to be no reason why it should employ a less efficient combination of factors as its output increases, or therefore suffer a rise in average costs of production. We must therefore pick up a loose thread by disclosing that our supposition does not always hold good, and that an industry as it grows may encounter the difficulty of a *scarcity* of one or more factors. There are two main cases to be considered, which I call 'Pigovian' and 'Shovian' increasing cost respectively, after the two Cambridge writers who have done most to elucidate them.

The first case occurs when the units of the factor are all alike in efficiency, or if they differ in efficiency differ *equally* from the point of view of our own and of other industries; e.g. if while some land is better than other, it is equally better for wheat-growing, barley-growing, pasture, etc. It may nevertheless happen that our industry is so large, and/or makes such specially large use of this factor, that as it grows in size it creates a perceptible shortage of the factor elsewhere. In this case, as our industry expands, the price of all units of the factor in every use will rise: our industry will have to pay more not only for the extra amount of the factor which is required for the additional output, but for all units of the factor which it employs. An instance is wheat-growing in a largely agricultural country.

The second case is perhaps more important, and also more complicated. The units of the factor may differ in efficiency when used in our industry, but be alike when used in other industries (two pieces of land may be equally good at cabbages, but one much better situated for building on): or they may be alike in our industry but differ in others (the same example will serve if we shift our viewpoint to cabbage-growing). Or again they may differ in efficiency in all uses, but differ by more in our industry than in others or in others than in ours: in the extreme case they may differ *in different directions* in our industry and in others. For instance if the demand for domestic service were to expand and that for cotton cloth to contract, one would expect to find the former 'industry' taking on women who are less and less suited to be servants and more and more suited to be cotton weavers.

In all these cases, as output expands in our industry, the cost of additional units of output will go up, since they are being produced with the aid of bits of factor which are progressively less efficient in proportion to what must be paid to attract them from other industries, – their so-called 'transfer price'. It might seem at first sight that there is no reason for the money costs of the other units of output to be affected. This, however, is not so: for in a competitive market the owners of those bits of factor which are more efficient in proportion to their transfer price will be able to ask a higher price for their use from the organisers of industry, whose costs of

H

production will thus be raised for all units of output. These extra costs are clearly of a peculiar kind, different from the costs necessary to attract bits of factor from other uses: they may be called 'producers' surpluses', and sometimes, at the risk of confusion, it may be convenient to call them 'rents'.

For any given scale of output, the cost of that part of the output which it is just worth producing contains no elements of this kind, but consists entirely of sums which must be paid to attract the factors employed from other uses. Thus we find a sense in which price may be said to equal 'marginal costs', – marginal costs excluding producers' surpluses, but average costs including such surpluses.

(2) DECREASING COST

Reasons for a falling curve are of a different order, and may be summed up loosely as economies due to the ingenuity of man. These may occur even when on balance the curve of average costs is rising owing to the influences just discussed, in which case what is about to be said of them still remains valid. Conversely, the supply curve of an industry, while falling, may not be falling as fast as it would be if the cost-raising influence of scarce factors was not in some degree present.

While other treatments have been proposed, notably by Mr Shove in the articles listed, we may, I think, conveniently follow tradition in distinguishing between 'internal' and 'external' economies of large-scale production, defined as those which depend respectively on the individual firm being large and on the whole industry being large. But it is important to note that, so defined, the two classes are not mutually exclusive.

Thus among external economies we have
(1) the whole mixed bag of things which is commonly

listed under this head (see especially Marshall, IV, 10), such as the growth of subsidiary firms making machinery etc., the establishment of markets for raw materials and finished products, the presence of a skilled labour supply and of a general atmosphere of shop. Some of these economies depend on the industry being *localised* as well as large; though with the improvement of communications these are perhaps of declining relative importance.

An analytical difficulty of which much has been made is that some external economies – e.g. improvements in transport and banking – due to the growth of industry A also lower costs in industries B, C, etc., so that while the products of A fall in *price*, they do not fall, or fall so much, in relative *value*, and our assumption that the two can be treated as identical becomes illegitimate. Or, what seems to come to the same thing, the demand curve for A cannot lawfully be treated as independent of its supply curve. Fortunately, we have also

(2) the important fact that as the scale of an industry expands, specialisation on the part of individual firms becomes easier and the costs of each firm therefore lower, – the whole 'industry' may even dissolve in a complex of 'sub-industries' engaged on different varieties of the same 'product' or different stages of the productive process (see especially the listed article by Allyn Young). And finally, we have

(3) the fact that as the industry expands each firm may become not only more specialised but larger, i.e. may find itself able to reap more of those internal economies of large scale to which we are coming in a moment. It is here that the overlap occurs between the two types of economy, – the lowering of costs is directly due to the firm's own expansion, but the firm wouldn't have expanded if the whole industry hadn't done so.

These internal economies (for a full discussion of which see Marshall, IV, 11, and also Robinson's *Structure of Competitive Industry*) may in their turn be conveniently divided in thought into two classes:

(1) those which arise because a large fixed plant or organisation is required in order to produce *any* unit of product (e.g. a railway), so that average costs fall rapidly as output is expanded and the costs of this fixed item are spread:

(2) those which arise from improvements in organisation or equipment which entail more elaborate division of labour between men and machines, and which are therefore worth making for a large output but not for a small; these normally require *time* for their introduction. These again may be classified into

(*a*) economies of *technique*, dependent on the size of the establishment, – the individual factory or shop;

(*b*) economies of *control*, dependent on the size of the *business unit*, – e.g. bulk buying and marketing, large-scale dealing with banks, division of labour in the higher ranks of control, – one partner or director dealing with sales, one with production, one with finance and so forth. These economies do not usually reach their limit so soon as (*a*), – one firm may well own many factories or shops.

It will be seen that in many of the economies of both main classes (i.e. external and internal), the element of *time* is of supreme importance. This fact has raised many doubts as to whether in such cases it is sensible to attempt to think at all in terms of a 'true' or 'conditional sentence' supply curve. Can we really, even if we are careful to correct for the effect of major inventions which clearly did not depend on the scale of the industry, ever hope to get beyond what is really simply an historical record of the way costs have fallen as output has risen? Certainly Marshall was very much alive – more so than several of his more mathematically minded but less mathematically competent successors – to the perils of the whole method (see V, 12, especially pp. 460–1 and Appendix H). We must, I think, concede that any curve we can construct is not perfectly reversible, i.e. that the cost per unit set against an output x should properly be less if output has shrunk to x from some higher figure y than if it has reached x for the first time, since not all the economies of specialisation won in passing from x to y will be lost in passing back from y to x. And the prospect of deriving such curves with success from the confused data of real life seems to be more remote than in the case of demand curves. Nevertheless, after a period of revolt,[1] I am now of the opinion that the concept of a true falling long-period supply curve is one which we cannot do without, though we must handle it carefully.

The next question is, Can such a curve still be falling at a point of competitive equilibrium, so that if the demand curve rises equilibrium will ultimately be restored at a lower price? Common sense and observation suggest the answer yes, but there are analytical difficulties. In facing them it will be convenient to use a mechanism invented by Pigou in 1928 and now part of standard doctrine. With this mechanism we peer for the first time into the cost structure of the individual firm. Now even when an industry is in equilibrium a firm may not be, – it may be rising or decaying. But we shan't learn much by looking at such a firm, and we therefore fix our eyes on one which is 'representative', – its characteristic from our present point of view being that if the industry is in equilibrium so is this firm, i.e. the state of the industry is the same as it *would* be *if* the industry consisted entirely of firms of this kind. Its conditions of cost are shown in the figure, where CM is the fundamental curve showing the successive additions made to total cost as output expands, – the curve of 'marginal cost'. CA is the companion curve of average

[1] The curious may care to see *Economic Journal*, January 1924, pp. 16–30, reprinted as No. 7 of *A.E.A. Readings in Price Theory*.

cost per unit of output, such that for any scale of output OR we have TORQ = CORV.

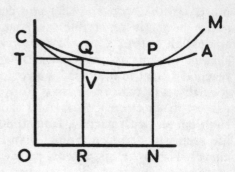

The position shown commends itself to common sense. CM starts by falling owing to the presence of indivisible lumps of factor, including the entrepreneur himself; so of course CA falls too. But after a point, even allowing for the gradual installation of larger plants etc. (for remember this is a long-period curve), CM turns upward, owing to growing difficulties of co-ordination and management. Over a range CA still goes on falling, and then, by a blessed dispensation of mathematics,[1] easy to test for oneself, turns up where CM crosses it, i.e. minimum average cost is attained when average cost equals marginal cost. Now for the industry, and hence this representative firm, to be in equilibrium, price must equal average cost, otherwise producers would be attracted to or repelled from the industry, and output would expand or contract. And for this firm, and hence the industry, to be in equilibrium, price must equal marginal cost, for if it exceeds it there will be an inducement to the firm to expand, if it falls short of it to contract, output. Hence, for equilibrium, price must equal PN and output ON, – the condition of equilibrium for the industry is that demand price should equal average *and* marginal cost of the representative firm, and that the latter's organisation and its proportion of its total output – in other words the number there would be of such firms if

[1] Let $x=$output, $a=$average cost of x, $b=$average cost of $(x+1)$. Then marginal cost of $(x+1)=b(x+1)-ax=x(b-a)+b$. This is $>$ or $<b$ according as b is $>$ or $<a$.

all firms were actually like this one – should be such that this is true.

It seems to follow that if pure internal economies were the only ones, we should have to conclude that in competitive equilibrium they must have ceased to operate. For if this were not so, the individual firm, finding the price in excess of its marginal cost, would go on expanding at the expense of its neighbours, and any firm which once got a start would secure a complete monopoly.

Pigou, sticking closely to his mathematics, accepts this conclusion, and for the explanation of competitive equilibrium under decreasing cost turns to external economies, in the extended sense of that term which includes the tendency of firms to reorganise, and above all to specialise more closely, as the scale of the industry grows. For as a result of this, the curves of the individual firm will be shifted downwards throughout their length. They may also so change their shape that their point of intersection is displaced to the right, i.e. the firm may become able to take more advantage than previously of the internal economies of large scale. But however that may be, at the new point of equilibrium price is again equal to marginal cost, so that there is no tendency for the representative firm to swallow its neighbours.

Marshall, in his intentionally looser and less precise treatment (IV, 13, and V, 12), lays stress on the rôle of external economies, but also on what seems to be a separate point. It takes *time* to reap most even of the internal economies of large scale, and before any actual firm had time to grow, it might have lost its luck or its vigour, so that not it but some other firm did the growing. The firm which is representative this year will have ceased to be representative next year; and 'the' representative firm, as it figures in the argument, is not some particular firm whose name is to be found in the directory, but a succession of firms, rather in the same way – to vary Marshall's own metaphor of the trees of the forest — as a wave which travels over the ocean consists in succession of a number of different collections of waterdrops. I believe that this picture makes an important contribution to the whole complex truth, though, as Marshall himself admitted in his 8th (1920) edition, the kind of situation which it illustrates had by then become less typical than it had been thirty years before.

Finally, Marshall lays stress on a more obvious point, undoubtedly very important in practice. In real life, the individual firm's costs include costs of marketing, — i.e. both of transporting goods to the market and of bringing them to the notice of consumers by display etc. — and it is very likely that the marginal costs of these processes will begin to rise sharply while those of actual production are still falling, so that the upward turn of the marginal cost curve is due to the former overbearing the latter. Now if the scale of the industry were to expand just by accident, as it were, there would be no reason for these marketing costs, for any given scale of output, to be lowered; but if — which is the case that really interests us — it expands as a result of a raising of the demand schedule, they may well be lowered; for now the individual firm can expand its output without incurring heavy costs for invading the territory, literal or figurative, of its rivals. Hence for this reason too, as the industry expands, the marginal cost curve will be lowered and shifted to the right, — the economies of mass production will get fuller play, and in the new equilibrium price will settle at a lower level than in the old. But in discussing this possibility we have really already left the domain of 'pure' competition, and we shall have to return to the matter later in a wider context.

Meanwhile one final word about the nature of the long-run competitive supply curve. Our discussion has shown that it is a rather more tricky thing than our original definition of it, and proposition about it, might have led us to expect. Under decreasing cost, as output expands average costs fall: but the reason they fall is that the industry has adapted itself to meet a raised demand schedule. Thus there is really the ghost of a demand curve passing through every point on the supply curve: the point, as it were, only acquires real existence if the demand curve *does* pass through it. We must not speak as if a casual lowering of price will evoke an expansion of output, – it will, as always, induce a *contraction* of output, while a casual raising of price will induce an expansion. Were it not so, the cardinal rule of value, by which it exercises its sway over the composition of the national output, would be falsified.

Thus if we look back at our two sets of conditional sentences expressing the conditions of supply, we find that the second set – 'if x is the output, a is the average cost per unit', etc. – can stand with a minor correction; we had better say 'average cost per unit in the representative firm', – not necessarily exactly equal to the arithmetical average for the output of the whole industry. But the first set needs filling out in some such way as this: 'if a were the price offered, x would be the output, *provided that* experience showed that not less than x was demanded at the price a', etc. Or again, putting the same thing in a slightly different way, we can define the long-period supply price of an output x as 'the price the expectation of obtaining which for the whole output x will just suffice eventually to evoke that output'.

X

MONOPOLY

In mentioning marketing costs, we have really abandoned
out model of 'pure' competition. Let us then turn to our
secondary standard of reference – absolute monopoly
(Marshall, V, 14). Literally speaking, this exists when
there is only one seller of the 'thing' or 'commodity' in
question; but it must of course be remembered that the
boundary line which we draw round a 'commodity' is to
some extent arbitrary, and that even a firm selling 100
per cent of the output of what we are choosing to call a
'commodity' may be in active competition with the producers of other 'commodities' which are more or less close
substitutes for his own. Further, we must not worry
about small divergencies from completeness; and what
may be called 'effective monopoly' may be said to exist
when one seller or group of sellers controls so large a
part of a trade – perhaps 80 per cent is a plausible figure –
as to be able to dictate successfully the level of price or
output. Between this extreme, or quasi-extreme, of effective monopoly and that of pure competition there are
many intermediate phases, to which we will return.

I must pass briefly over the questions of the origins
and structure of monopoly. It is perhaps convenient to
distinguish three types of monopoly classified by origin,
though there is much overlap; these are (1) legal, (2)
natural, (3) organisational. (1) Monopoly may be founded
on *legal privilege*, as it was under the Tudors and Stuarts,
notably in the case of the great trading companies, but
also in other fields. 'Our loving subjects,' we read, 'who
have long complained of the bad and stinking soap now
ordinarily in use, shall have good, sweet and serviceable
soap for their money', – a quotation which illustrates that

monopoly powers have often been accorded, ostensibly at least, on grounds of public interest, – generally on the ground that this is the only way to get a difficult or risky task effectively taken in hand.[1] In modern times we have such examples of legal monopoly as the B.B.C. and now British Railways, the Coal Board, etc.; and an element of legal privilege enters into the monopoly position of some manufacturing companies whose strength is based partly on the grant of exclusive rights to operate patents, – an institution which, though it cuts both ways, has been held on balance to further the progress of invention and research.

(2) Monopoly may come about *naturally*. Here we may distinguish (*a*) cases where the sources of supply are limited and localised – salt, potash, quicksilver, diamonds; (*b*) industries making use of a large distributive plant which it would be obviously wasteful and inconvenient to duplicate – the so-called 'public utilities', or as I have called them 'octopoid' industries, of gas, water, electricity and so forth; and (*c*) ordinary manufacturing industries where the internal economies of large scale are very pronounced. In spite of what has been said earlier, such economies do often, especially since the legal invention of the joint-stock company made it easy to collect and to preserve from dissipation great masses of 'command over capital', tend to eventuate in monopoly; and in my view some latter-day exponents of the merits of *laissez-faire* have erred in underestimating this tendency and in over-stressing the part played by Governments, great as that has often been, in smoothing the road towards monopoly.

(3) Finally, monopoly may come about as a result of *combination*. This, however, is itself often facilitated by (2*a*), the localisation of scarce resources; or again is often the outcome of 'cut-throat competition' between large

---

[1] Monopolies were also granted to make spangles and to print the psalms of David, as well as for the possibly more lucrative enterprises of making paper and importing steel.

quasi-monopolistic bodies which have evolved as a result of the exploitation of the economies of large scale (2*b* and 2*c*). Among monopolies which take the form of combination a broad distinction may be drawn between those where combination is confined to the processes of marketing and sale, and those where it extends also to the actual processes of production, – this distinction corresponding broadly to the popular labels of 'cartel' and 'trust' respectively. But within each group there is a vast variety of financial and organisational arrangements whose study belongs more properly to a descriptive course on the structure of industry and will not be pursued in these lectures.

I turn therefore to the pure theory of monopoly. The monopolist, unlike the purely competitive producer, will be in a position to make a gain in excess of normal profits: and we will begin by assuming that he will so act as to make this gain – his net monopoly revenue – as great as possible. In pursuing this object he will take into account, as the competitive producer will not, the effect of increasing his output (1) in lowering the price of all the units which he sells; (2) in increasing the producers' surpluses and perhaps also the transfer prices which he will have to pay to the hired factors of production; but also (3) in lowering his costs owing to the reaping of economies arising from the growth of the whole industry, – economies which would have been 'external' to the competitive producer become 'internal' to him. Taking all these into account, he will, on our present assumption, push output to the point at which his net monopoly revenue is a maximum, or, in other words, at which his 'marginal receipts'[1] are equal to his marginal costs, – the former being defined as the addition made to his sales proceeds

---

[1] I prefer this phrase to the more commonly used 'marginal revenue', since the quantity in question is the marginal increment of *total receipts*, not of *net income*, and the word 'revenue' to me suggests *income*.

by an extra unit of sale, account being taken of the fall thus occasioned in the price of all units sold.

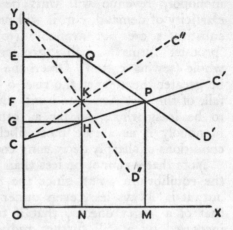

The diagram illustrates the simple case in which the curves of demand and cost are straight lines, i.e. in which the same absolute change in amount demanded is associated with each 1s reduction in price, and the same absolute change in amount produced associated with each 1s increase in average costs. In this particular case, the monopolist's output will be one-half what it would be if he carried on up to the point at which the price just covered his average costs.[1]

Both in this particular case and in the more general one of convex and concave curves, the ratio of monopoly price (QN) to marginal cost depends on the elasticity of demand at Q, the relation being[2] that price is equal to marginal cost multiplied by $\dfrac{\eta}{\eta - 1}$, an expression which is greater the less is η. Given the cost curve, the net

---

[1] If the curves are like this ⟩ it will be more than a half; if like this ⟨ , less than a half.

[2] The algebraic proof is as follows: Let x = output, $\phi(x)$ = price. Then η, expressed as a positive quantity, is $-\dfrac{\phi}{x\phi'}$. In equilibrium marginal cost = marginal receipts; and marginal receipts $= \dfrac{d(x\phi)}{dx} = \phi + x\phi' = (1 - \dfrac{1}{\eta})\phi$; or ϕ = marginal receipts multiplied by $\dfrac{\eta}{\eta - 1}$. Let those who prefer geometry see J. Robinson, *Economics of Imperfect Competition*, p. 36.

monopoly revenue will thus be greater the less the elasticity of demand, e.g. it will *pro tanto* be great where substitutes are not available (tobacco) or where the 'product' forms a small ingredient in a more complex whole (sewing cotton). Given the demand curve, it will be greater the steeper the rise, or the more gradual the fall, of the cost curve, and will thus – fortunately – tend to be least where, so far as other considerations go, monopoly is as a rule most likely to arise, i.e. under conditions of sharply decreasing cost.

Note that η cannot be less than one at or to the left of the equilibrium point, since the total cost of a smaller output is always less, even under decreasing cost, than that of a larger one, so that if total receipts could be increased by a still further reduction of output, so *a fortiori* could monopoly revenue, and Q would not be a point of equilibrium. Note too that the damage done to the consumer through the monopolist not carrying output as far as M consists not in the higher price *per se* – the consumer is ex hypothesi paying for the Nth unit what it is worth to him – but in the destruction of consumers' surplus (the area EFPQ).

If we could suppose that the monopolist's average cost curve was identical with what the supply curve for the whole industry would have been under pure competition, we could express these results in terms of a direct quantitative comparison between what happens under monopoly and what happens under pure competition. But in some cases, e.g. the 'public utilities' already mentioned, it is really impossible to conceive of the industry being conducted under conditions of pure competition; in others it is likely that the monopolist's cost curve will differ in various ways from what the industry's supply curve would have been had competition continued to prevail. On the one hand he may be able to reap economies of large scale, for instance of large-scale research, which would have been beyond the reach of an assemblage of competitive producers, and also perhaps to avoid paying certain ground rents or other producers' surpluses which they would have had to pay. So far as these things are true, his curve will be below the competitive supply curve; and output, even if he is acting in such a way as to maximise monopoly revenue, will be greater than it would otherwise have been, and *may* even exceed competitive output. This will, of course, be the more likely if the monopoly extends to the unified organisation of production than if, like a trade association or some forms of cartel, it merely exercises control over price and scale of output. On the other hand it is all too likely that in some cases the monopolist will *not* reduce costs in ways in which they might have come to be reduced had competition prevailed. According to many observers, the main damage done by monopolies to consumers arises not so much from restriction of output below the level which, with existing cost conditions, competition would establish, as from what one critic has described as 'the suppression and discouragement of new methods in the interests of already established capital'.

When we turn from examining a stationary position to examining the effects of *change*, there is a further difference between monopoly and competitive conditions to be noted. Under competition we can be sure that, if supply price is rising, a raising of the whole demand schedule will lead to a rise in price, and, if supply price is falling, that it will lead to a fall in price. But under monopoly the dependence of price on elasticity of demand, enshrined in the formula $\dfrac{\text{price}}{\text{marginal cost}} = \dfrac{\eta}{\eta - 1}$, prevents us from being sure of what will happen when demand increases unless we know what has happened to the elasticity of demand. E.g. if the new demand is much less elastic, at the old price, than the old, the new price may be higher than the old even if the curve of marginal costs is a falling one.

All these matters are discussed very clearly and elaborately by Mrs Robinson (10–14).

We have so far been assuming that the monopolist is in fact acting so as to secure the maximum monopoly revenue. But it is of great practical importance to remember that he may not in fact always, or perhaps even ever, be acting in this way. The motives which restrain him from doing so may be mixed and perhaps not always clearly apprehended or formalised by himself; but it is perhaps possible to discern among them four separate strands.

(i) He may fear *potential* competition and desire to avoid being put to the trouble and expense of crushing or buying out a competitor. When, however, monopoly springs from economies of large scale, it may in practice be so difficult for a new man to set up on a scale that really threatens the monopolist's position that the deterrent effect on the monopolist of this possibility is not very great. Where monopoly takes the looser form of trade association or cartel, the fear of a break-away by the low-cost members may sometimes be pretty effective in exercising a restraining influence on the price policy of the group.

(ii) The monopolist may desire to nurse and develop his market for the future, – he does not take his existing demand curve as immutable, but seeks to raise it by judicious behaviour. But of course there is always the risk that such a period of nursing will come to an end, and the monopolist decide that the moment has come to reap the harvest of his previous self-control.

(iii) The monopolist may well find it a nuisance to be continually manipulating his price in response to every movement in demand. Thus he may well be acting 'more monopolistically' when demand is low than when it is high, and less monopolistically over the two periods taken together than if he had been intent on reacting to every change. In effect he will be taking part of his monopoly reward in the shape of a relatively quiet life.

(iv) Finally, in a society still mainly competitive, where the feeling that price *should* equal cost is still strong and vocal, the monopolist may well be actuated by a general sense of decency, shame or fear of public opinion. This influence must certainly not be underrated, though it is naturally apt to grow more feeble as monopoly grows commoner and receives, as has tended to happen in this country till quite recently, a greater degree of Government support and legal protection.

The upshot seems to be that witch-hunters into the abuses of monopoly power come back oftener than one might expect with empty hands: but that nevertheless the problem of the treatment of monopoly remains one of the most difficult and pressing problems of the modern State. For the present, however, we must stick to analysis, and eschew prescription.

XI

MONOPOLISTIC COMPETITION

We must now enter the jungle lying between pure competition and effective monopoly. It seems most convenient to describe the whole of this jungle as 'monopolistic competition', though the name has been reserved by various writers for various parts of it. The jungle contains some of the most difficult tracts of theoretical and practical economics, and we can do little more than peep into it. Let us do so with the aid of certain models which have been found useful in attempting to understand the complexities of the real world.

We may start with one which, to judge from examination papers, is still very popular in Cambridge, though, as we shall see, it has some manifest drawbacks. It purports to represent what is sometimes called 'polypoly in an imperfect market'. There are a large number of sellers, but the buyer is not indifferent from which of them he buys: each seller has a limited and conditional monopoly depending on the fact that some buyers are bound to him by geographical propinquity, by rational or irrational preference for his particular brand of the 'product', or simply by sheer force of habit. The seller thus finds himself confronted with a sloping demand curve, – he does not expect to lose all his customers if he raises his price, nor to be able to extend his sales indefinitely if he lowers it. Since his rivals are numerous, he assumes that nothing he does will appreciably affect the actions of any one of them, nor therefore react back on his own prospects; i.e. he takes this individual demand curve as a known and definite thing. Nor does he attempt to operate on it so as to change it in any way. Finally, there is supposed to be no special difficulty about entering the trade, so that the level of profit prevailing in it cannot for long exceed that prevailing in the rest of industry.

We may impound some of the difficulties connected with time, differences of ability, etc., by carrying over into this model the device of the representative firm. The position in such a firm, when the industry is in equilibrium, is shown in the diagram (see Chamberlin, p. 76). The number of firms in the industry has become so adjusted that the firm's individual demand curve lies tangent to its curve of average costs, i.e. no abnormal profit is being made, and there is no tendency for additional firms to be attracted to the industry. But since the demand curve is a 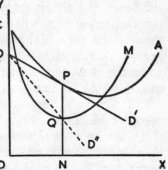 sloping one, the point of tangency lies to the left of the lowest point on the average cost curve. Price thus stands in excess of marginal cost, just as it does under true monopoly: if the firm attempted to expand output towards the point at which they would become equal, it would drag down the price of all previous units of sale, and would no longer be able to cover its total cost as it does at P. We can, if we like, drive in the point by drawing in the, marginal receipts' curve DD″ and showing how it cuts the marginal cost curve at a point directly beneath the point of equilibrium.

This model serves well enough to bring out three important facts about the world of 'monopolistic competition'. (1) Price is higher and total output less than under pure competition. (2) The individual firm is not carrying output to the point at which its production cost per unit of output is at a minimum, – there are unexhausted economies of large-scale production, which is prima facie wasteful, − though *how* wasteful we had better suspend judgment. (3) As under true monopoly, the question of what happens to price when demand increases depends partly on what happens to the elasticity of demand. For instance if, when demand increases, a number of new firms enter the market in such a way as to loosen the bands of custom which bind consumers to the old firms, the elasticity of demand for the product of the representative firm will increase, and price may fall even though the marginal cost of the new scale of output is greater than that of the old.

At the same time there are some peculiarities about the model which are not always fully appreciated.

(1) The assumption that while existing firms find considerable difficulty in invading each other's markets there are no special obstacles to entering the trade from outside, and hence no 'monopoly revenue', seems rather a queer one. There may be activities in real life, retail trade perhaps among them, to which it corresponds better than at first sight appears probable. But as a rule one would suppose that the *time* which, in ordinary competitive theory, is needed to bring to fruition competition from outside, would also operate to undermine the special attachments supposed to exist within the trade and to flatten out considerably those individual demand curves. Or that if it did not avail to do that even in the long run, neither would it avail to break down the barriers in the way of entry, so that we should get something more like a position of true monopoly established, with a level of profits permanently above that prevailing elsewhere. In the hands of some of its more enthusiastic exponents, the theory of so-called imperfect competition sometimes seems to halt rather confusingly between being a short run theory and a long run theory, according as its eyes are turned inwards or outwards.

(2) The model leaves out altogether what is, in the

real world, the most obvious
sign that the market for a
thing is imperfect, namely
that the sellers are incurring
all sorts of costs of packaging,
display, advertisement, etc.,
in order to maintain or extend
the demand for their particular
variety of the thing. It even
leaves out the cost of trans-

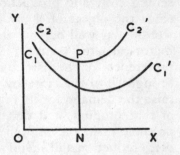

port to the market, at any rate so far as the market
is scattered; i.e. the average cost curve which is falling
at the point of equilibrium is really a curve of production
costs *at works*. We can get nearer to real life by super-
imposing, as Chamberlin does, a curve of the selling costs
necessary in order to dispose of varying quantities of output at a given price on the curve of production costs.
This curve of selling costs is likely to fall in the early part
of its course, with the economies of large-scale organisation of selling operations and with the cumulative effect
of assaults on the consciousness of the individual consumer; but it is bound to rise after a point as new customers
have to be sought and as increasing 'sales resistance' is
encountered from old ones. And the combined curve of
production and selling costs (C_2C_2'), unlike the curve of
production costs alone (C_1C_1'), must be at its minimum
at the equilibrium level of output: i.e. this point is one
beyond which it will not be worth the firm's while to
attempt to extend its market by incurring increased
selling expenditure any more than by cutting the price.
For a full diagram illustrating this situation see Chamberlin, p. 148: in the partial extract here given note that the
selling costs included in the combined curve C_2C_2' are
those of marketing various quantities of product *at the
price NP*.

There still remains the difficulty that the line between

selling costs and production costs may be hard to draw, since the object of many even of the costs incurred 'at works' may well be – notably for instance in the case of a motor-car – to maintain or enhance the consumer's preference for the particular 'make'. But this too can be brought into the story by recognising that the firm can raise the demand for its product by altering the character of that product, and that it will pursue this method of product variation, as well as the other two methods of price reduction and selling expenditure, up to what seems to it to be the margin of profitability in each case. As an excellent illustration of the way these things really do happen, see this account[1] of how Cadbury's cut down its selling expenditure in order to bring up the weight of the 2d bar of chocolate to exactly two ounces – a very solid type of product variation to which the most austere advocate of utility production could scarcely take exception! – and of the startling increase in sales which resulted.

(3) The third dubious feature about the model with which we started is that in supposing each seller to be confronted with a perfectly definite demand curve, it slides over the question of how he expects his rivals to react to his own actions. If those rivals are very numerous, this may be regarded as a fairly plausible simplification; but it can scarcely be so regarded if they are few, or even if, being fairly numerous, they are arranged, so to speak, not at random, but like lines of upright dominoes radiating outwards from himself, so that a push administered by himself will have a considerable effect on the nearest member of each line, be transmitted by him to the next member and so on. Under conditions of this kind the principles of what is called 'oligopoly' have got to be brought into the story.

By oligopoly is meant a state of affairs where the sale of a product is in the hands of a few large independent

---

[1] *Industrial Record*, pp. 35–8 [handed round the class].

sellers, each of them acting monopolistically in the sense that he is taking account of the effect on price of variations in his own output. What will happen to price and output under such conditions? Unfortunately the answer is not too clear, having been indeed a matter for debate in the most highbrow circles for many decades! To cut short a story which I am by no means qualified to tell in full, it seems that we can conduct our reasoning on any one of four separate suppositions, and shall reach different results accordingly. (i) The first supposition, which was that made by Cournot when he set this ball rolling in 1838, is that each seller assumes that, whatever he does, his rivals will not alter their *output* to counter him, but will continue to sell for what they can get. In this case it can be shown[1] that the price and output will be determinate at a point intermediate between the monopoly and the competitive levels, approaching the latter more nearly the greater the number of competitors. (ii) The second supposition (made by Cournot's critic Bertrand) is that each seller assumes that his rivals will not alter their *price* whatever he does, but will continue to sell, at the old price, as much or as little as they find that they can. In this case each of them will start price-cutting against the others, and equilibrium will be reached, even in the extreme case where there are only two sellers, at the competitive level of price and output.

In point of fact, however, neither of these suppositions, in spite of their distinguished history, seems very plausible; for it seems natural to suppose that if each seller is himself conscious of his power of affecting price by means of output or sales by means of price (whichever way we like to put it) he *must* be aware that the other sellers are conscious of the same power and may be expected to use it. Each seller indeed, and this (iii) is the

[1] See Chamberlin, Appendix A; and, on this whole subject, Pigou, *Economics of Stationary States*, chapters 16–17.

third supposition, may be so certain that if he cuts price or expands output the others will follow suit that he is restrained from doing so; in this case, without any actual collusion between them, price will settle at the full monopoly level, with output contracted accordingly. On the other hand – and this is (iv) the final supposition – each seller may be so uncertain as to precisely how the others will think he will behave, and how consequently they will behave themselves, that the whole situation is clouded with indeterminacy and instability, leading perhaps to alternations of price-wars and uneasy truces, – as seems often in fact to have been the case.

So much for true oligopoly, i.e. the case where the sellers are really very few in number. In the less spectacular case from which we started, i.e. in which an element of oligopoly, in the sense of concern about your competitors' probable reactions, leavens the situation described as polypoly in an imperfect market, the natural inference seems to be that price will probably be higher and output smaller, and both perhaps less stable, than where that element is absent. In some cases wasteful expenditure on advertising and so forth may be avoided, since everybody fears to provoke reprisals by embarking on it. But in accordance with the general assumptions of the polypoly model, it is not to be inferred that the gain from higher prices, or the saving on selling expenditure, will materialise in permanent monopoly profits; there remains the alternative, so long as entry to the trade is unhindered, of their being slopped away in higher costs due to the human and material agents of production not being used up to their full capacity.

There remains, however, yet another possibility to be mentioned, namely that each seller should expect a different degree of reaction from his rivals according to the *direction* in which he moves his own price. Thus it may be that, a given price and output situation having once developed, each seller fears that if he cuts prices his rivals will follow suit, so that he won't gain anything, while if he raises prices his rivals *won't* follow suit, so that he will lose a good deal of his trade, — a rather complex but not unplausible state of mind which can perhaps be described as oligopolistic pessimism, since it involves expecting the worst of both worlds! In this case the individual demand curve with which the seller conceives himself as confronted may be represented as kinked at the established point of equilibrium, being pretty elastic to the left and relatively inelastic to the right, — the elasticity of the right-hand portion being more or less

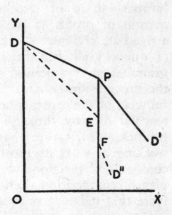

identical with that of the curve for the whole industry, i.e. each producer reckons that if he lowers price he will be allowed to get 'his share' of the trade but no more. In terms of margins, the marginal receipts curve is discontinuous at this point, taking the course DEFD", and there is a considerable range over which either the demand curve or the marginal cost curve might shift without affording any ground for altering price.[1]

This apparatus is used by Hall and Hitch in their important article (see list, p. 31) as part of the

[1] An arithmetical illustration may help some people:

Output	Price	Total receipts	Marginal receipts
1	100	100	100
2	99	198	98
3	98	294	96
4	90	360	66
5	84	420	60
6	78	468	48

explanation of the observed fact that entrepreneurs frequently do not conceive or represent themselves as striving to equate marginal cost and marginal receipts at all, but rather as setting and maintaining a price which covers full average costs of production, including a 'proper' share of overhead costs and a 'reasonable' margin of profit. If we ask exactly how this price is arrived at, 'the nearest we can get to an exact statement' (I quote Hall and Hitch, venturing to correct their grammar at two points) 'is that the price ruling where these conditions obtain is likely to approximate to the full cost of the representative firm; and that this price is reached directly through the community of outlook of business men, rather than indirectly through each firm working at what its most profitable output would be if competitors' reactions were neglected, and through the play of competition then varying the number of firms'. Note that it is the representative firm's costs (including profits) that are taken as basis by the other firms, i.e. the sub-normal firm is not regarded as setting its price at a level which would yield normal profits. A price so arrived at is likely to be pretty stable over periods of considerable length, though, as Hall and Hitch admit, (1) entrepreneurs may be knocked off it, both upwards and downwards, by extreme movements of demand, (2) it is liable to be disrupted eventually by a change of technique on the part of some existing firm or by the irruption of an enterprising outsider. The Hall and Hitch model is thus perhaps a contribution to a medium run rather than either a true long run or a very short run theory of value.

The work of Hall and Hitch has been carried on by a group at Nuffield College, of which Mr Andrews is the leading, if not the most lucid, member (see listed articles by him and Miss Brunner). The picture they now paint is of a number of independent producers all setting and working to a price which is based not so much on their own actual costs of production as on what they believe to be those of an efficient – actual or potential – competitor, including what for him – not necessarily for themselves – would be a ' proper' margin of profit, – this being the price which experience shows that, for that scale of output in the industry as a whole, the consumer will pay.

There has been much discussion on how far this picture is in contradiction with, and how far it is reconcilable with, that which represents the individual producer as seeking to maximise his *long run* profits in an imperfect market and being prevented by competition from obtaining a profit above the normal level. Opinion seems to be coming round to the view that there is not so much difference as might be thought at first sight. And perhaps, if we remember the greater elasticity of most demands in the long run than in the short, there is not so much difference between either and the pure theory of competition, interpreted with due regard to the time factors on which Marshall laid so much stress. Indeed having hacked our way through the jungles of oligopoly, polypoly, pliopoly and what not, we seem to find old Marshall, representative firm in hand, standing to welcome us on the other side! And by his side stands his pupil Pigou, reminding us[1] that 'the maximum principle operates upon human beings, not upon electrical machines of perfect sensibility', so that people sometimes act 'according to the rule of competition' even though the abstract conditions for pure competition are not perfectly fulfilled.

[1] Loc. cit., p. 88. For further discussion, see the listed articles by Machlup and myself.

XII

THE SHORT PERIOD

Marketing costs caused us to slide from competition into monopoly. In a somewhat similar way, let us allow Hall and Hitch to help us to slide from the long period into the short (Marshall, V, 5), – reverting however, to start with, to full competition.

A short period is defined as one in which there is time, in response to a movement in demand, for a firm to vary the rate of output from its existing plant, but not time for it to alter the scale of the plant itself; nor for new firms to set up new plants. The word 'plant' is used in a broad sense to include both the physical equipment of buildings, machinery, etc., and the organisation embodied in a nucleus of salaried officials, research workers and so forth.

The concept of short period is thus a fluid one, since some elements of the plant can be expanded or contracted more quickly than others. Moreover the short period is not, so to speak, the same length at both ends; the length of time which it takes to create equipment is generally shorter than its length of life when created, so that a rise in demand will react more quickly on the scale of plant than a fall, – an important fact apt to be obscured in a period of rapid progress.

Simplifying unduly, as so often, for the sake of precision, let us consider the behaviour of an individual firm – assumed, as before, to be representative – in the 'short period'. Its full costs can be thought of as made up of two parts, – the fixed or 'supplementary' costs of maintaining the fixed plant, whose total amount will be unchanged whatever the output and indeed even if there is no output at all, and the variable or 'prime' costs whose total amount will be zero if there is no output and will be larger the larger the amount of the output. Let us look at each a little more closely.[1]

From the point of view of the responsible heads of the firm the fixed costs will be of very different kinds. Some of them, such as salaries, will have to be paid somehow at the due dates if the firm is to keep running efficiently;

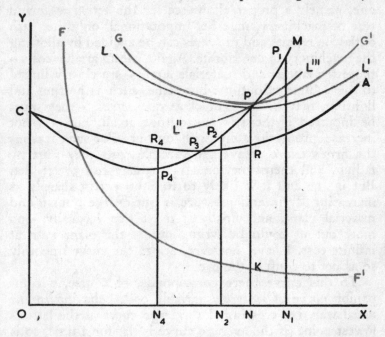

others, such as interest on debt, will have to be paid unless special legal arrangements are made to the contrary; others again, such as allowance for the obsolescence of machinery or profits for the owners or ordinary shareholders, need not be paid out in cash at all. But they all have this in common, that their amount does not depend

[1] I think the account which follows owes a good deal to a (still unpublished) dissertation by Professor R. F. Kahn.

on the volume of output. In the picture the fixed costs per unit of output are represented by the curve FF', which is such that the rectangle contained by it (e.g. ON × NK) is the same size for every point on the curve.

The variable costs again are of different kinds. Most of them, namely those of labour and raw materials, involve more or less immediate cash payments; but one important one, namely a proper allowance for the actual wear and tear of machinery, may be 'imputational' only, i.e. cash outlay on repairs and renewals can be avoided by allowing the machinery to deteriorate. Again, most variable costs – those for labour and materials again – are closely linked to the volume of output: but some, such as heating and lighting, may be thought of as quasi-fixed, – they must be incurred if there is any output at all, but will not increase proportionately with output. For such reasons the firm's curve of average variable costs may start by falling, and thereafter for a range may run pretty flat. But in the end it is likely to turn up pretty sharply as increasing strain and pressure is put on the human and material plant, and finally it must rise vertically, – no more output could be wrung out of the plant even at infinite cost. I have, however, drawn the curve smoothly so as not to confuse the eye.

To this curve there corresponds, of course, a companion curve of *marginal* variable cost, behaving in the usual way, i.e. crossing the average curve at the latter's lowest point (if the average curve is flat for a time, so is the marginal curve; and like the average curve it ends by going straight up in the air).

The pure theory of competitive short-period equilibrium states that the output of any firm will be carried up to the point at which price (assumed, as in long-period competitive theory, to be independent of the firm's action) is equal to the firm's marginal variable cost: provided only that at this level of output price is not below *average* variable cost, – for, if it is, as at P_4, it will prima facie pay the firm to shut down rather than produce anything at all. A firm's marginal variable cost curve can, therefore, to the right of P_3, be regarded as its short-period supply curve; and a large-scale replica, so to speak, of a 'representative' firm's marginal variable cost curve constitutes the short-period supply curve of the whole industry (e.g. if the representative firm is of such a size that if all firms were the same size there would be 500 of them in the industry, the relevant part of CM will serve for the short-period supply curve of the industry if we treat ON as standing for 500 times as much output as it does in the case of the representative firm).[1]

Going back to the firm, I shall use the ugly word 'global' to signify the sum of average variable and of fixed costs. Average global costs are shown on the picture by GG', – thus, for instance, PR = KN. If the output, determined in the manner just explained, happens to be that to which the scale of the plant is adapted, that means that average global costs are at a minimum, and total global costs are just being covered by total receipts (ON × NP). If P lies higher up than this on CM, as at P_1, they will be more than covered, and an abnormal profit made; if lower, as at P_2, the firm will not be covering its fixed costs, – though of course this may mean no more than that it is failing to make a normal profit. If P lies at the intersection of CM and CA (i.e. at P_3), no contribution at all is being made towards meeting fixed costs, – if some of them are nevertheless being met, it must be out of capital resources or borrowed funds.

One more point before we stand back to look at the model in the light of real life. What is the relation of GG' to that curve of average costs which we found in Chapter 9 intersecting its marginal companion at the point of

---

[1] [A critic points out that this assumes a perfectly elastic supply to the industry of the variable factors.]

long-period equilibrium? Even that curve, you will recall, was not exactly a 100 per cent long-period curve, — we found we might have to redraw it (and of course its marginal companion) as the scale of the whole industry changed. But it *was* a long-period curve in the sense that it assumed that the firm was free to vary the scale of its plant, and was in fact always working with the most appropriate scale of plant. The answer then is that our new curve GG′ lies on the top of our old curve LL′ like a small bowl lying inside a larger one. What this means is that (1) in full equilibrium the firm is both using the most suitable scale of plant and operating it to the most suitable degree of fullness; (2) if it were to increase output, average cost would rise more sharply than if it had time to increase the scale of the plant, since it would be imposing on the plant a degree of pressure for which it was not designed; (3) equally for a decline in output average cost will rise more sharply if the scale of plant cannot be reduced than if it can, since each unit will be bearing a share of the fixed cost of an unnecessarily large plant. Looking at the picture, it will be seen that the point P is a regular Clapham Junction, — through it pass the curves of long-period average cost, long-period marginal cost, short-period average global cost, and short-period marginal variable cost (which is the same as short-period marginal global cost); only short-period average variable cost is left out in the cold!

Now let us stand back from the model and ask how much light is thrown by it on the conditions of real life. There seem to be three things to be said.

(1) Short-period equilibrium, like long-period equilibrium, is at best something which tends to happen, not something which is always, or indeed perhaps ever, actually happening. The obstacles to its establishment may be less formidable than in the case of long-period equilibrium, but they exist, — obstacles caused by Nature

and technique, by time and ignorance. There has, I think, been a tendency to forget this in some modern work, and to treat short-period equilibrium theory as a satisfactory substitute for the dynamic analysis of processes of change. But to this I will return, apropos of fluctuations in the whole economy, later in the year. Subject to this caution, it is evident that the model is a helpful tool.

(2) In times of depressed demand, price *may* in some cases fall more and output less than the model suggests. For (i) by neglecting variable costs – notably wear and tear of plant – which do not have to be met in cash, and carrying output further accordingly, a firm can increase the excess of cash receipts over cash outgoings on account of variable costs, and thereby perhaps evade bankruptcy by paying bank interest or some other fixed cost which has to be met in cash. This is what is known commercially as 'weak selling'.(ii) If price is such that the least unprofitable output would cause a 'prime loss' (e.g. P_4N_4, causing prime loss of $P_4R_4 \times ON_4$), this output may nevertheless be produced, since the loss may be less than the costs involved in shutting down and opening up again; it costs a large sum per month to keep a ship laid up, and a large sum to bring back into blast a blast furnace which has once been blown out, – in a sense even a nil output has its variable costs.

(3) This example of the blast furnace serves to remind us that momentary considerations are not the only ones that count, even in the short period. As regards manufacturing industry, much the commonest case in real life seems to be that in which, in a time of depressed demand, price is *not* driven right down to marginal variable cost, and output is reduced more than our model would suggest. In ordinary language this result is due to the individual producer's fears of 'spoiling the market'. Such fears are partly *directly* self-regarding, – fear of glutting the market and so making it harder to sell later, fear of frightening

K

the consumer into holding off buying or making him think he has been cheated in the past. But partly they are due to a corporate instinct — though this too, as always, may be *ultimately* due mainly to self-regard; there is a strong feeling that price 'ought to' cover full costs, and strong resentment against a blackleg who cuts prices unless he is absolutely compelled.

All this means of course that even in what appear to be highly competitive trades producers do not usually act, when demand is temporarily depressed, in a fully competitive manner. In some cases they take account, in accordance with the principles of 'polypoly in an imperfect market', of the influence of their own output on price; in some cases they take account further, in accordance with the principle of oligopoly, of the probable effect of their own behaviour on their competitors' behaviour. We can give a rough idea of the result, as Marshall suggests (pp. 374–7), by portraying each producer as retreating, when demand falls, not along his marginal variable cost curve but along a curve lying above it and containing some allowance, arrived at in a more or less arbitrary manner, for fixed charges; and we can conceive, as Marshall does, of a short-period supply curve for the industry compounded of such individual curves. Modern analysis, with its formidable jargon, has endeavoured to give greater precision to these results. Some of its exponents have perhaps overlooked the emphasis with which Marshall more than sixty years ago hammered in, in the passage just referred to, the main truth that long-period considerations enter strongly into the determination of short-period value and output. If, however, we think it corresponds better with the facts, we can recast the whole apparatus to fit the assumptions of 'polypoly in an imperfect market', i.e. of the representative firm finding itself chronically faced with a sloping demand curve. In this case our LL′ and GG′ will still lie tangent to one another, but not at their minimum points. In long-run equilibrium the representative firm will be producing with less than the most economical size of plant, and will be working that plant at less than its full capacity (see Harrod, listed articles).

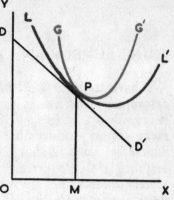

XIII

JOINT SUPPLY AND PRICE DISCRIMINATION

We have hitherto kept fairly closely to the simplifying assumption that a firm produces only one 'product'. But it is evident that in real life a firm – for example a mixed farm – often produces habitually a large variety of things which by no stretch of language can be described as forming a single product, i.e. which minister to completely different needs. What is to be said about the forces determining the value of each of them and the length to which its output will be carried?

It is customary to start with the extreme case in which two or more things – say two for the sake of simplicity – are produced in proportions which cannot be altered, – e.g. as the result of a chemical reaction or a process of botanical growth. In this case it is not possible to isolate the separate cost of one of the products. Marshall indeed (who deals with these matters in V, 6–7) being always concerned to emphasise the connection of value with cost, suggests that even in this case we can attach a legitimate meaning to the cost per unit of A; it is, he says, arrived at by taking the total cost of the whole productive process for any given scale of output, deducting therefrom the total receipts from the sale of B, and dividing the remainder by the number of units of A. There is perhaps no great objection to this, but I think no great advantage in it either. In any case the points of substance are (1) that in full competitive equilibrium the aggregate receipts from the sale of both products must cover the aggregate costs of their joint production (including of course a normal profit); (2) that an increase in the demand for A is bound to lead to an increase in the output of B and so, given the demand for B, to a fall in its price.

But such rigid conditions do not generally prevail except in the short run. More usually, given time, it is possible to vary the proportion of the two things in accordance with the relative strength of the demands for them. Let us take the time-honoured case of an alteration in the breed of sheep designed to meet an increase in the demand for mutton, that for wool remaining unchanged. The matter can be put in two different ways, which at the limit come to the same thing. You can estimate how much less wool you would have to produce, and how much money receipts you would therefore have to forgo, in order to produce an extra wad of mutton without any change in your total expenditure. Or you can estimate how much you would add to your total expenditure by producing an extra wad of mutton while keeping the amount of wool produced unchanged. The sum arrived at in either of these ways, divided by the number of units of mutton in the wad, may be called, in a rather peculiar sense of the words, the marginal cost of mutton; though Marshall, in his latest formulation of the matter (*Industry and Trade*, p. 193), seems disinclined to go further than saying, in a very characteristic phrase, that this sum 'may in some sense be taken as indicating' the cost of mutton! Normally the marginal cost, so calculated, of a joint product will increase as its output is extended, since the difficulties in the way of further substitution will grow more formidable (even the meatiest sheep must be allowed some wool or it will die of cold); and the output of each product will be carried to the point at which its marginal cost is equal to the marginal addition to receipts derived from its sale, – which of course, in the case of pure competition but not otherwise, is equal to its market price. The concept of the total or average cost of wool alone, or mutton alone, still has no precise meaning; but competition, so far as it is at work, will still tend to prevent the total receipts from wool and mutton combined from exceeding, or falling short of, the total costs of sheep-farming.

Where conditions of this kind prevail, it is not absolutely certain that a rise in the demand for one product, say mutton, will lead to an increase in the output of the other (wool) and so to a fall in its price. For the rise in the demand for mutton will exercise two conflicting influences, one tending to increase the number of sheep produced and the other tending to decrease the proportion of each sheep that consists of wool; and it is not impossible that the latter influence should outweigh the former. But it is not likely to do so if the increase in demand is at all large, since, as already stated, the difficulties of substitution are likely in most cases to grow pretty rapidly with every extension of the scale on which it is attempted.

If, however, in any particular case substitution is very easy, — so easy that from the producer's point of view the two products, even though meeting different needs, are virtually one product, we reach a situation closely analogous to that which, in the case of a single product, is described in the books as 'composite demand'. Composite demand exists when the same thing is required for a number of different purposes, — as for instance coal for use in gasworks and for use in ships. An increase in the demand for coal due to an increase in the demand for gas will tend to *restrict* the supply and *raise* the price of coal in the shipping use and so to restrict the supply and raise the price of the service of sea-transport. Thus the principles of joint supply and composite demand can be regarded, if we like, as half-brothers. Both arise from the same underlying situation, — the possibility of meeting two or more needs from a common source; but according as the one or the other element predominates in any given situation, an increase in the urgency of one of the needs will lead to the other need being *more* full, or *less* fully, satisfied.

Let us look a little more closely at those cases where the technical possibilities of substitution by the producer appear to be very great, i.e. where there appears to be no physical necessity, as there is in the case of mutton and wool, to produce *any* B if you produce *some* A. In the first place it is worth noting that the necessity is sometimes greater than it appears to be at first sight, since the production of A at one *time* necessitates, or at all events is greatly facilitated by, the production of B at some other time. This evidently explains a good deal of what happens in agriculture under systems of rotation of crops; the roots which clean the soil for the wheat in the following year may be said to be being jointly produced with the wheat in almost as strict a sense as the mutton with the wool. And we can perhaps extend this principle to the case where production has to adapt itself to seasonally changing demands, as in the celebrated instance of the Luton hatmakers, who started making straw hats because the Bedfordshire straw is so good and naturally turned to making felt hats to keep their plant and labour-force occupied in the winter.

So far we have not necessarily any conflict between the existence of joint supply and the existence of pure competition; but this last case of seasonal demands brings us very close to the case, obviously very common in real life, where one firm is turning out *simultaneously* a large number of different things although there is no physical compulsion to do so. There is, for instance, to take an example not from manufacture but from retail trade, no physical need to sell cheese if you sell candles, but many shopkeepers do so. It is sometimes said that these are merely cases of *common* cost, the costs e.g. of the rent of the shop being common to both products, and not of joint cost at all; but the distinction, though sanctioned by Marshall and Pigou, does not seem to be very watertight. The truth rather seems to be that while there is no *physical* need to produce the second product (I continue to speak for simplicity as if there were only two, though of course there are often many), there is a *commercial* need to produce either it or some other, since otherwise the fixed costs of the business could not be covered. This brings us back to our old friend the limitation of markets. If you could count on selling unlimited amounts of cheese or candles at a given price, it would presumably be more sensible, even if more boring, to sell cheese only or candles only: and in a large town something of this kind, in some cases though obviously – *vide* Woolworths – not in all, tends to happen. Thus joint supply in this broader sense is bound up with the causes which make markets imperfect. At the same time, somewhat paradoxically, it helps to set bounds to their imperfection. For (to carry on with the example from retail trade) if each of three or four village shops can easily stock a number of additional lines at only small marginal cost, that will make it harder for any one of them to obtain anything like a local monopoly in the sale of any one product – the demand curve with which each of them is faced will become more elastic. But this greater perfection of the market for each product does not alter the fact that in such situations, owing to limitation of the market, the plant of each firm is not being used in the most economical conceivable way.

When *this* kind of joint production – or if we prefer it 'common production' – prevails, the business of calculating the marginal cost of each separate product, for the purpose of weighing it against marginal receipts, becomes a very tricky one. Much labour and ingenuity is often spent by cost accountants in attempting to attribute to each product, on top of its direct cost in labour and materials, a supplement to allow for any specially great use which it makes of the machinery, the storage space, the selling organisation or any of the other elements of the fixed 'plant' of the business. This seems reasonable enough: what is not so clear is that it is reasonable to start, as the accountants often do, by allocating to each product a basic share (calculated as a rule as a percentage of direct costs) of the fixed costs of the business, before going on to indulge in the further refinements just described. Marshall takes this procedure as a matter of course:[1] some later writers have been disposed to condemn it as a piece of meaningless and misleading superstition.[2] To me it seems a reasonable thing to do as a guide to long-run action. For in the long run, at least, the alternative to producing one of these 'common products' is not to produce nothing but to find something else to produce; and the decision to abandon a particular line of production is akin to a decision to leave one 'industry' for another, — a type of decision to the making of which, as we have seen earlier, it is the level of average, not of marginal, cost which is relevant. This seems to be the sort of way in which these 'loaded' estimates are in fact used by practical business men. Thus Neal (*Retail Trading*, Chapter 13) describes how in a large department store each item displayed for sale is charged at the beginning of the season with a carefully calculated 'initial mark-up', but in many of them 'mark-downs' are accepted if the event shows it to be necessary as the season proceeds. Any line, however, on which heavy mark-downs had to be consistently accepted season after season would presumably be discarded and replaced by another which it was hoped would achieve better results.

Thus we seem to end up with something of a paradox. On the one hand joint production in the extended sense, alias 'common production', is less compatible with a purely competitive situation than is joint production in the stricter sense. But in a way it conforms more closely

[1] 'In cases of such common or allied production, each thing is charged with a share of those expenses which are incurred on account of the general work of the business' (*Industry and Trade*, loc. cit.).

[2] See, for instance, Cairncross, *Introduction to Economics* (second edition), p. 275.

to the plain man's idea of competition, in that under it there is a stronger tendency in the long run for the price of each product to conform to something which can sensibly be thought of as its full separate cost of production.

For the sake of completeness I must here add a word about the companion pair of half-brothers, joint demand and composite supply. Joint demand exists when two or more things are required to fulfil a single purpose, as are whisky and soda-water. Composite supply exists when a single need can be satisfied from two or more sources, as the need for artificial light can be satisfied by gas or by electricity. My – not very original – illustration of joint demand is taken from the realm of consumers' goods; but its most important applications arise in connection with the derived demand for the factors of production, and it will be convenient therefore to examine it more fully later in connection with the theory of distribution. Enough for the moment to say that up to a point the analogy with joint supply is close. Thus in the extreme case in which the proportion in which A and B are required is rigidly fixed, there is strictly speaking no determinate desiredness (to use a general word to cover both consumers' goods and factors) of A or B alone, though if we like we can speak of the marginal desiredness, measured in money, of A as being the difference between the marginal desiredness, measured in money, of the whole caboodle and the cost of B. But when, as is more usual, the proportions can, given time at least, be altered, we can, as we saw earlier when examining the principle of substitution and the law of diminishing return, attach a separate marginal desiredness to each of them. Analogously again with joint supply, a lowering of the supply schedule of A will have a double-edged effect on the demand for B, tending to raise it through extending the quantity of the whole caboodle demanded, and to lower it through setting the principle of substitution at work, — the net effect depending on the relative strength of the two influences. For instance if people are almost indifferent as to whether they drink their whisky and soda strong or weak, provided it contains *some* soda-water to give it a fizz, a fall in the price of whisky might actually diminish the demand for soda-water and lower its price. Thus at this end of the scale the principle of joint demand has affinity with the principle of composite supply; for it is evident that in the case of composite supply proper a cheapening of one alternative — say gas — will tend to lower the demand for, and so the price of, the other alternative — say electricity. More commonly, however, where joint demand prevails, a cheapening of A will on balance raise the demand for B.

The 'principle of joint supply', in the sense of the predominant influence on price of the relative intensity of *demand* in different markets, applies under certain conditions to different portions of the same 'thing' as well as to different 'things'. Indeed I have already illustrated this in the instance which I gave of 'commercial joint supply'. For it is really simply a question of words whether we speak of the retailing of cheese and the retailing of candles as 'different things' or as the sale of 'the same thing', viz. the service of retailing, in different markets.

Let us, however, look more closely into the matter. The first question which arises is, what are the conditions which make it *possible* to sell 'the same thing' at different prices in several different markets, — let us say, for the sake of simplicity, in *two* different markets? Those conditions are two. (i) It must be impossible, or at any rate too expensive, for purchasers in the cheaper market to transfer the thing to the dearer market. That is why price discrimination is commonest in the case of services, — one cannot hand on an operation for appendicitis. But the condition may sometimes be fulfilled in the case of goods, especially as between home and foreign markets. Sale abroad cheaper than at home is facilitated by the high cost of re-import, reinforced perhaps by duties or prohibitions. Or – a less common case, but one illustrated by British coal after the first world war and again today – sale at home cheaper than abroad is made possible by prohibition of unauthorised export. (ii) It must be impossible, or at any rate not worth while, for the purchaser in the dearer market to transfer himself to the cheaper market. As Pigou points out, it is not worth while becoming poor in order to get cheap operations. A less obvious instance is this. The cost of providing first-class accommodation by rail is greater than that of providing second class; nevertheless, if the difference in cost is less than the difference in charge, the first-class passenger is being discriminated against. But he cannot escape the discrimination except by giving up the comfort of first-class travel, and experience shows that there are a certain number of people who do not find it worth while to do so. Much the same applies to different-priced seats in a theatre.

The next question is, is price-discrimination ever compatible with pure competition? At first sight it would seem not – each competitor will believe himself able to sell an indefinite amount in the dearer of the two markets, and his efforts to do so will bring the price to uniformity. But this does not hold where joint supply in the stricter sense prevails, so that a firm cannot supply market A without also supplying market B. A road haulier cannot supply transport from London to Cambridge without supplying transport from Cambridge (directly or indirectly) to London, or all his vans would bank up in Cambridge. A Cambridge lodging-house keeper cannot own a source of accommodation in term without owning a source of accommodation in vacation. In such cases it seems that even pure competition would evolve a system of discriminating prices. And we can note the important conclusion that in such cases an increase in demand in market A will increase supply and lower price in market B. For instance, a recovery in our ability to export coal would tend to lower the freights on imported food and raw material.

But as in the case of 'different things', so in the case of 'the same thing', the principle of joint supply is also frequently found in operation when the compulsion to serve more than one market is not physical but commercial, — there is no other way in which the fixed costs of plant and organisation can be covered. That is the situation which I have already illustrated from retail trade; and as we have seen it is not one of 'pure competition', though it may tend to *resemble* competition, first in that fair freedom of entry to the trade checks the making of monopoly profits, and secondly in that elaborate costing sometimes tends to produce a closer link between long-run full cost and value than might at first be supposed.

Such cases in the real world shade into those in which a firm, in a position anyhow to make monopoly profits, is also in a position to increase those profits by splitting the market. In the extreme theoretical case in which the monopolist could charge a separate price not only to each customer, but for each unit sold to any customer, he could collar the whole of what would otherwise become consumers' surplus; and it would pay him to expand output right up to the point at which demand price equals marginal cost. In the picture (which will be used again and hence contains more lines and letters than are needed for this particular exercise) CC' is the curve of average, CC'' of marginal, costs. The acquisition by the monopolist of powers of perfect discrimination enables him to turn the demand curve into a curve of marginal receipts and to increase his monopoly profit from the area GCFQ to the △ DCQ'.

Actually in the real world he will have to be content with more or less rough and ready groupings, and try to maximise his monopoly profit in each market so formed, – if we like, to carry sales in each market up to the point at which his marginal receipts in that market equal the marginal cost of the whole output.

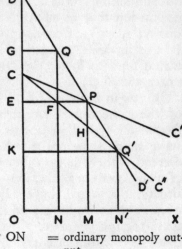

ON   = ordinary monopoly output

GCFQ = ordinary monopoly revenue

ON'   = discriminating monopoly output

DCQ' = discriminating monopoly revenue

It is not so easy as one might perhaps expect to say whether his *output* – as contrasted with his profits – will be increased by the exercise of such partial or rough and ready powers of discrimination. But broadly speaking the truth seems to be as follows.[1] If the market is split into two parts, a dearer part and a cheaper part, it may be that the new cheaper part consists *entirely* of persons who would have made no purchases if the market had not been split, or it may be that it consists only partially of such persons. In the latter case total output *may* be increased as a result of the splitting, but in the former case it *must* be. And if it *is* increased, and if decreasing cost prevails, price will be lower in *both* markets than it would have been if there had been no discrimination. This is an important

---

[1] For further analysis, let those with fairly strong stomachs see Pigou, II, 17–18, and App., pp. 808–10; and those with *very* strong stomachs, J. Robinson, 15–16.

conclusion. It means for instance that a cartel which sells cheaper abroad than at home will very probably sell cheaper at home than one which is compelled to sell at the same price abroad and at home; and that a railway which charges less per ton-mile for carrying coal than for carrying furniture will probably charge less for carrying furniture than one which is compelled to charge the same for carrying coal and for carrying furniture. In some cases, moreover, permission to discriminate will enable an enterprise, for instance a railway, to be started when otherwise it would not have been, there being *no* uniform price sufficient to yield a normal, let alone a monopoly, profit.

Whether, however, price-discrimination is on balance socially desirable cannot of course be finally decided without reference to what alternative is envisaged: and to that we shall return.

XIV

SOME DEFECTS OF ECONOMIC FREEDOM

I have so far tried to explore the working of the theory of value with a minimum of critical appraisal. I want now briefly to consider and classify the chief ways in which its operation in a régime of economic freedom may lead to a distribution of productive resources between employments which falls short of producing the best results in terms of economic welfare: and to consider also, though even more briefly, possible remedies.

(1) Even under a régime of pure competition, there are a number of miscellaneous reasons for which the costs incurred by an individual entrepreneur may fall short of the full costs imposed on society by his productive activity. The stock instance – and it is still a good and important one – is the damage and expense inflicted on a whole neighbourhood by the smoke from a factory chimney. If all these costs could be evaluated in money and loaded on to the industry which causes them, that would make it considerably less profitable than it is. When such incidental damage is technically inevitable, we may say that the use of resources in the industry which causes it is being carried further than the public interest dictates; where it is remediable, it is perhaps more illuminating to say that the use of resources in remedying it is not being carried so far as the public interest dictates.

The converse case also occurs. It may be that expenditure of a certain type by an entrepreneur, e.g. by a farmer on land drainage, would lower the costs of others beside himself, but, since he would not reap the whole benefit himself, is not carried so far as the general interest demands. Such disharmonies can often be resolved by *co-operative* action, – co-operation, as we pointed out to our Martian long ago, is one of the possible manifestations of economic freedom. But these cases shade off into those, typified by defence and public health and also already noticed in an earlier lecture, in which *communal* consumption, financed by levy, is the remedy to which even the most individualistically minded societies are inevitably led.

(2) Still adhering to the model of pure competition, I come to a more technical matter. In approaching it, let us suppose first that in the bulk of industries in competitive equilibrium there are no unexhausted economies of large-scale production. Then, if in some particular industry there *are* such unexhausted economies – if the supply curve either *is* sloping downwards or *would* be sloping downwards but for the cost-raising influence of some scarce factor – then prima facie production is not being carried so far in that industry as the public interest dictates. If means could be found to carry it further, for instance with the aid of a subsidy, economies could be reaped at the expense, so to speak, of the devil, – there would be an increase of consumers' surplus with no corresponding increase of social cost.

This, however, is to put the matter a little too simply, in three ways. (i) It is conceivable that all or a majority of a country's industries should be in this position, and in this case it would not be possible, since the supply of productive factors is limited, to expand all of them to an appreciable extent. More generally, we must amend our statement by saying that output is prima facie too small in those industries in which the economies of large scale are greater than the average and too large in those in which they are less than the average. (ii) In drawing inferences about practical policy, we must, I think, remember the reasons – so much stressed by Marshall and so apt to be obscured in ultra-mathematical analysis – for supposing that the reaping of the economies of large scale is largely bound up with the passage of *time;* and we must not be too ready to suppose that intervention can effectively do that leisurely old gentleman's work for him. (iii) In so far as the economies of large scale are irreversible, a temporary rather than a permanent subsidy may suffice.

If there were reason to suspect the prevalence of increasing cost in an industry due to analogous causes, i.e. to *dis*economies of large-scale production, there would be an analogous case for checking the growth of such industries. But instances of this are hard to find, or to invent. As a rule, increasing cost is due to factor-scarcity of one of the types which I have already described as Pigovian and Shovian, i.e. *either*, as the industry expands, it has to pay higher transfer prices for all its supplies of some factor on which it makes specially great demands: *or* it has to pay higher transfer prices for some bits of factor, while other bits of the same factor, which are relatively more efficient for the purposes of this industry, are thus put in a position to exact producers' surpluses. But in either case this change in the price of factors has come about as the result of an expression of consumers' preferences in the form of money demand, and there is no prima facie case for going behind it or attempting to set aside its consequences. The increased incomes represented by the increased money costs represent a mere handing over of wealth from consumers to the owners of the scarce factors or bits of factor. There may be reasons for regretting this, but they are of a different order from those now under consideration, and point to collaring or taxing these surpluses (if you can find a way of doing so) rather than to restriction of the scale of the industry in which they occur.

Thus the asymmetry in the causes of decreasing and increasing cost leads to a corresponding asymmetry in their implications for public policy.

(3) More obviously important is the conclusion that

where, in a mainly competitive world, certain industries are in the hands of monopolies, output in those industries will – provided the monopolists are actively exploiting their powers – not be carried so far as the public interest dictates. In the face of this situation the State may adopt various policies, the full discussion of which belongs to 'applied economics' rather than to 'economic principles' – they are discussed admirably by Pigou (II, 20–1), and doubtless by many of your lecturers, and I shall do no more than classify them briefly. (1) The State may content itself with acting on the aphorism 'Light is the sovereign antiseptic and the best of all policemen', – with enforcing publicity about costs and profits, and trusting that shame or fear will do the rest. (2) If the tendency towards monopoly is judged not to be irremediable, it may attempt to combat it directly by prohibiting the formulation of mergers, price-fixing arrangements, etc.; or it may attempt to keep the field open for potential competitors by proscribing certain methods of trading designated as 'unfair'. Such are, for instance, arrangements of various kinds which tie the customer to the monopolist by forcing him to go to the monopolist for *all* his supplies – e.g. shipping services, the use of machinery – if he goes to him for *any* of them: or intensive selling campaigns at less than economic prices which the small competitor cannot possibly stand up against. (3) If monopoly is adjudged inevitable, the State may administer direct control of prices and/or profits, – one objection to this being that in order to be well-informed and effective such control may involve a large duplication of administrative machinery. The analytical point is worth noting that if the monopoly is working under conditions of increasing cost, the fixing of price at the competitive level will not of itself induce the monopolist to increase output up to the competitive level, since he can reduce his payments of producers' surpluses by stopping short of that level (for geometrical discussion see Pigou, p. 807). (4) Finally, the State may operate the monopoly itself, either directly or through some kind of semi-independent commission or corporation. This of course raises the question of how far in practice public monopolies are likely to be free from the defects – especially the defect of a tendency to suppress new methods – exhibited by private ones: as well as more political questions such as the advisability of having large bodies of voters who are directly or indirectly employed by the State and in a special position to bring pressure on it.

It belongs rather to my province to develop a point which was first made by Marshall many years ago (p. 489), though its full implications have only been generally realised in more recent times. It is really the same point as I have already touched on in connection with competitive industries conducted under conditions of decreasing cost. Where monopoly is the result of large internal economies of large-scale production – as especially in the case of the 'octopoid' or public utility group of industries – the presumption is that output should be expanded not merely up to the point at which price just covers average cost, thus yielding a normal instead of an abnormal profit, but right up to the point at which price just covers *marginal* cost, even though that involves production at a considerable loss. For only thus will the maximum excess of additional consumers' surplus over financial loss be attained. In the picture on p. 160, the expansion of output from OM to ON' will increase consumers' surplus by EKQ'P and cause a financial loss of CKQ'. The difference between these two areas is the $\triangle$ PHQ' (since, with straight-line cost curves, the $\triangle$ CEF = the $\triangle$ PFH).

To secure this result it might be necessary that the industry should be publicly owned and operated, since it would be difficult in practice to subsidise a private monopolist *on condition that* he acted in this way. And in some cases it might be right for the State to set up an industry and operate it on these lines, when otherwise it would never have come into existence at all, since for all output demand price falls short of average costs, though not, for all output, of marginal costs. This seems to have been the sort of case Marshall had in mind in the passage referred to, – e.g. an irrigation work set up by a Colonial Government.

And it is worth noting a point made by Mrs Robinson, – namely that so far as this principle of equalisation of price with marginal cost can be applied in monopolistic industries, the need for attempting the more difficult task of applying it in the case of competitive industries subject to decreasing cost is diminished. For many of the external economies of large scale in manufacturing industry resolve themselves into the *internal* economies of large scale to be reaped in 'octopoid' or other ancillary industries.

All the same, there has been a tendency, to my mind, in much recent economic literature to play this principle for somewhat more than it is worth. Many writers take it for granted that publicly owned industries should certainly be operated on this principle; and some even seem to suggest that the fact that an industry offers scope for the application of the principle should be regarded as a decisive argument for its being publicly operated. Neither of these things is self-evident. There are a number of other considerations, especially of course those concerned with efficiency of management, to be taken into account in deciding whether or not an industry should be publicly operated. And if it *is* to be publicly operated, the public interest may be better served on balance by a common-sense rule that it should, over a cycle of years at any rate,[1] at least cover its full costs, than by a rule that it

[1] 'Taking one year with another', as the British Nationalisation Acts say – though experience seems to show that 'taking one half-century with another' might have been a more appropriate phrase.

should produce at a loss up to the point at which price equals marginal costs; since this latter rule might be very difficult to combine with any practical test of efficiency of management. A right distribution of productive resources between employments is a 'good thing' economically, but not the only good thing, even economically! (See Wilson's listed article.)

Further, while the gain of consumers' surplus PHQ' *is* a net gain, it is a net gain which is only secured by altering the distribution of income against the rest of the community and in favour of the consumers of the particular product, – electric light, rail transport or whatever it may be. The more such products there are, the less, perhaps, the force of this objection, since if there are many it might be expected that most consumers would benefit under some ticket or other. But by the same token the probability would be greater that the taxation necessary to pay the subsidies would, in view of all the other claims on the modern State, press heavily on the sources of enterprise, thrift and work.

In many cases, whether exercised by private hands or those of the State, the device of some variety or other of 'two-part tariff' – e.g. a fixed telephone rental plus a charge for each call over a certain number – would seem to be an acceptable alternative to subsidised production. For it combines the principle of equity – that the consumers of a particular service should between them bear its total cost – with the principle of economy, – that the most effective use of resources will be attained by carrying output up to the point at which price received from the sale of an additional unit equals the additional cost of producing it.

(4) Where, however, as in the case of railway transport, this device is not applicable, there is another which is. This leads me to my fourth heading, – the social merits and demerits of price discrimination. Generally speaking,

price discrimination is much resented. Even the instance of it which in the past has met with most approval – the charging of differential fees to rich and poor patients by doctors – is not particularly equitable; there seems no good reason – I speak feelingly – why the cost of removing the gall-bladders of the poor should be borne by the relatively rich man who has to part with his gall-bladder rather than by the relatively rich men who don't. From this point of view at least, a State medical service open to all and financed by taxation has advantages.

On the other hand, price discrimination, as we saw in Chapter 13, is often one way of reaping the advantages of large-scale plant and organisation; and merely to prohibit it without putting anything else in its place would lead to reduction in output, and in some cases to the ultimate closure, or to the non-birth, of enterprises prima facie meeting a social need. There seems therefore much to be said for sanctioning it in appropriate cases, subject to the condition that its results do not yield an abnormally great profit. This, in fact, is the policy which has long been pursued by the State in England towards the railways, – whose difficulty has been, both before and since nationalisation, to find a scheme of discrimination which will yield even a normal profit. I must confess that Pigou's discussion of the railway rate problem (II, 18) has never satisfied me very well. He seems to me to make a number of concessions which go far to emasculate his own argument, and then to end up by giving an unduly unfavourable judgment on the principle of discrimination, or 'charging what the traffic will bear'.

Nevertheless laudable attempts have been made since nationalisation, by more careful accounting, to fix charges more closely in accordance with cost. One difficulty is that if the consumer resents discrimination, he also often resents being charged according to true cost; e.g. the traveller on an unfrequented route in the Highlands 'does not see why' he should pay more per mile than the traveller by fast train from London to Edinburgh, though his journey certainly costs very much more. The consumer really needs a double process of education, — first to learn to accept the principle of charging according to true cost, and then to learn to accept departures from that principle! But in inculcating those lessons, it will probably be necessary, for political and social if not for strictly economic reasons, for the unhappy Transport Commission to avoid such unequal treatment of apparently similar individuals as too grossly offends the awkward human passion for personal justice.

(5) As with monopoly, so with 'polypoly in an imperfect market', if we find some industry which is subject to it in a world which is mainly competitive, there is a prima facie reason for supposing that the amount of resources engaged in that industry is too small. But here the chief trouble is rather that the amount of a particular kind of resource engaged, viz. independent entrepreneurship, is too *large*; i.e. that there are too many firms and that cost per unit of output could be reduced if control of the hired factors of production were concentrated in fewer hands. If, as is sometimes asserted, the whole or greater part of a country's industry is in this condition, then, as in the case of decreasing cost, we must modify our statement, and say that there are too many entrepreneurs and too few hired factors in the branches of industry where markets are more imperfect than the average, and too few entrepreneurs and too many hired factors in those where it is less imperfect than the average.

In applying this conclusion to retail trading, the most commonly cited case of market imperfection, we must remember that retailing is not so much an 'industry' as the end process of a number of different industries. Hence, it does not seem that the 'rationalisation' of retailing would necessarily lead to an increase of the hired factors employed in it. Nor of course would it lead to an increase of the hired factors employed in those industries purveying display and advertising facilities whose *contraction* it would be one of the main objectives of rationalisation to bring about. Rather the rationalisation of retailing might be expected to lead to an increase *both* of entrepreneurship *and* of hired factors in the earlier or productive stages of industry in general at the expense of the final or marketing stage.

We must, however, I think, be on our guard against exaggerating the benefits which would accrue from a ruthless ironing out of the consumers' preferences which cause markets to be imperfect. There is a real convenience in buying from a tobacconist 20 rather than 2,000 yards from one's door, – real spiritual comfort in buying a packet of a known and trusted brand of cocoa rather than a shovelful of brown powder of uncertain origin.[1] Chamberlin himself, who has often been regarded as the arch-counsel, so to speak, for the prosecution, in one passage of his original book (p. 94) went so far as to describe the situation brought about by natural forces as 'a sort of ideal', – the amount of diversity which consumers get is, he seems to concede, the amount they are prepared to pay for, and who shall say that they are wrong? And in a chapter (IX) added to later editions he has developed this point of view more explicitly, appearing as a champion rather than a critic of the 'monopolistic competition' which he analyses. Indeed he takes up a position which is a little too optimistic even for me, – there seem to me certainly to be some fields in which it is not in fact sufficiently possible to choose how much or how little 'selling effort' one will buy with one's purchase, whether that selling effort is embodied in the article itself in the form of decoration or gadgets, or whether it pervades the circumstances of its sale, as in the case of the superfluous amenities provided

---

[1] Mr. Kaldor's example, I think.

by some shipping companies and some large shops. More particularly in the case of intermediate products such as tools, and of minor ingredients and fittings, large economies of standardisation seem too often to persist unreaped, though here again good results can be and have been produced by voluntary co-operative enterprise. War-time experiments in 'utility' production of complete consumers' goods, though now mostly disappeared, will doubtless also leave a permanent mark on the commercial structure. But my own bias, as you have doubtless discovered, is to look with some suspicion on the sterner denouncers of the vices of imperfect competition, who want to make me walk a mile to buy my cigarettes and to flatten out all sorts of pleasant little pockets of consumers' surplus lurking under those – perhaps after all not so very steeply – downward sloping demand curves!